Praise for
The Primary Learner's Toolkit

An invaluable resource for any primary school teacher. It includes exciting innovative ideas, leading to creative work in the classroom. This toolkit is exceptionally user friendly and accessible to all teachers regardless of how long they have taught for – your students will notice if you use ideas from this text.

**Karen J. Duffy, Senior Lecturer Psychology,
Health and Social Science with Citizenship Education, Manchester Metropolitan University**

Most people know that children's school experiences need to be different to meet the needs of the current age. Jackie Beere shows how this can be done.

The Primary Learner's Toolkit is full of carefully thought out suggestions for the teacher and children as they seek to develop the learning habits that will bring success. The crafted activities that develop explicit techniques for learning in children are built upon a set of principles that help the teacher recognise the need to move their practice forward.

The structure practises the book's method of providing hooks for understanding to develop. The five habits are outlined and then expanded in ways that reflect recent thinking in SEAL and teachers who have been working on this agenda will be able to exploit this book.

For the teacher who wants young people who believe in themselves, organise themselves, think they can achieve, and endlessly push their own learning, this is a 'must read'… and 'must use' book.

Mick Waters, Professor of Education and President of the Curriculum Foundation

At last a book written for teachers that is easy to read and focuses on what the best education should look like in the 21st century. With or without the Rose Curriculum, I believe the development of personal, social and emotional learning skills is essential to develop successful learners for life. Jackie's book will help make the development of these skills manageable for teachers and the MAGIC acronym will be easily accessible and memorable for both children and grown-ups.

Gwynne Kynaston, Head Teacher, Burley Primary School

An easy to read, well set out book which inspires one to fully engage with the SEAL framework for primary schools in an imaginative and fun way. The book is split into four sections and includes projects and lesson ideas with teacher notes to accompany which assist the development of emotional intelligence.

Majella Kennedy, Senior Lecturer, Humanities Education, Manchester Metropolitan University

The Primary Learner's Toolkit

- Implementing a creative curriculum through cross-curricular projects
- Developing social and emotional intelligence
- Creating independent, confident and lifelong learners

Jackie Beere

 Edited by Ian Gilbert

Crown House Publishing Ltd
www.crownhouse.co.uk
www.crownhousepublishing.com

First published by
Crown House Publishing Ltd
Crown Buildings, Bancyfelin, Carmarthen, Wales, SA33 5ND, UK
www.crownhouse.co.uk

and

Crown House Publishing Company LLC
6 Trowbridge Drive, Suite 5, Bethel, CT 06801, USA
www.crownhousepublishing.com

British Library of Cataloguing-in-Publication Data
A catalogue entry for this book is available
from the British Library.

13-digit ISBN 978-184590395-4

LCCN 2009936676

Printed and bound in the UK by

Bell and Bain Ltd, Glasgow

Contents

Section II: Cross-Curricular Projects

Section III: The Stories

Section IV: Tools for Assessing and Tracking Skills

Foreword

Once upon a time a powerful man called Balls asked a man who had a bit of spare time called Rose to spend a lot of effort and money to go on a special quest.

The particular Holy Grail they were looking for was a magic formula that would turn little children into happy, confident and successful grown-ups in a world where everything was no longer what it used to be.

And all the magicians in the land, the alchemists whose job it was to turn potential into gold, were very excited not only because they thought that things were finally going to be better for everyone but also because they were being listened to. They hadn't had that for such a long time.

Not everyone was happy with what the man called Rose was finding and dark forces began to roam the land exclaiming loudly such things as 'Not enough Shakespeare!' and 'What, no Ancient Egyptians?' and 'Children to learn about blogging and climate change as government reforms relegate history in curriculum.' Even the great Prince became involved, exclaiming 'But what about teaching the history of my family?' and there was a great deal of gnashing of teeth and flapping of the *Daily Mail* by everyone who lived in Middle England.

Like a cowboy with sweaty palms, the man called Balls stuck to his guns and listened carefully to the special magical formula that Rose had discovered when he had talked to the alchemists of children. He then decreed that this formula should be known across the land and be made real in every school so that its magic be available to everyone.

And there was a great deal of rejoicing and cheers of 'About flipping time!' and 'Finally we can teach our children what they need, not what someone who has no idea about the specific needs of our kids in this community thinks they should have because that's what they had when they were at grammar school en route to a career as an accountant before they got a job in politics and it worked for them so that means everybody has to learn about those bloody Ancient Egyptians …'

Yet the dark forces were gathering strength in Middle England with their battle cry of 'Backwards into the Future!' striking fear into the hearts of all who heard it. How, the dark forces demanded, can we ever expect our future workers to be able to conduct high-powered business meetings with world-class executives from Brazil, Russia, India and China if they don't know who Miss Haversham is?* And one day it came to pass that the man called Balls ended up with only 1,121 more friends than his arch-rival and the very best friend of the man called Balls ended up with no friends at all and had to leave the palace to concentrate on his family and a public speaking career.

With that, darkness fell upon the classrooms apart from the glare of the interactive whiteboard with a PowerPoint about the Ancient Egyptians and silence fell upon the classrooms apart from the chanting of the six times table and all the effort and money that the man called Rose had spent were cast away and all the hope that was in the teachers' hearts was cast away and the most important opportunity to create a primary education system that was worthy of the 21st century and not just a recycled Victorian model was lost for another 1,000 years.

The End

* Kent grammar school educated ex-chartered accountant Conservative MP Nick Gibb addressing a Reform conference, London 2010. See www.guardian.co.uk/education/2010/jul/01/pupils-must-know-miss-havisham. For those of you who have never heard of Gibb or Miss Haversham, one is a bitter, angry and deluded middle-aged figure of ridicule who tries to stop time, forever hearkening back to an era when things were better and who admits to stealing young hearts and putting 'ice in its place'. The other is a Dickens character.

Postscript

There is a glimmer of hope from this terrible story though. The fact that people like Jackie Beere have shown time and time again that teaching children, not subjects, makes an extraordinary difference to their lives both in and out of the classroom.

By teaching children how to think, by helping them develop their emotional intelligence as well as their cognitive intelligence, by developing their creativity and communication, by focusing on how and not just what to learn, by all these things you end up with children who are better at learning (and 'achievement', the other Holy Grail of the powerful men and women) as well as who actually enjoy the process leading to better motivation and behaviour.

It might be magic but it's not rocket science.

This book, complementing so well the others Jackie has written in this area for older children, is designed to give the busy primary teacher everything they need to really bring the best out of their children as well as tick many boxes in important areas from the Social and Emotional Aspects of Learning (SEAL) agenda to the competency curriculum to Every Child Matters.

Who knows, it may even mean the difference between teachers teaching the Ancient Egyptians and children developing the skills, competencies and attitudes that will ensure they become fantastic lifelong learners who may just happen to have learned stuff about the bloody Ancient Egyptians.

Ian Gilbert
Clevedon
June 2010

Preface

Creating powerful learners within the primary curriculum

This book is intended to provide resources that deliver:

■ the crucial personal and emotional aspects of primary school education (Social and Emotional Aspects of Learning (SEAL))

■ the development of essential skills which were identified in the Primary Curriculum Review

■ the subjects of the national curriculum.

I have divided the book into four sections: Section I covers the 'MAGIC habits' that will help you to develop the learning and thinking skills so important for our 21st century learners; Section II comprises six projects that can act as a starting point for your work; Section III consists of three stories about Bobby Brain that reinforce the habits of social and emotional intelligence and provide good discussion opportunities; Section IV provides ideas and resources that will help you to help your learners assess what has been learned, what skills have been practised and, importantly, how it all happened.

The table overleaf summarises how the projects and lessons in this book cover the primary curriculum.

Using this book

Section I provides a detailed set of lessons which can encourage all the habits for learning. If you have not already done so, it is recommended that these lessons are worked through during – or in advance of – the projects in Section II as part of the delivery of SEAL or Learning to Learn provision. The impact of the project work will be more powerful if the learners have developed an understanding of their learning styles, preferences and how to develop their emotional intelligence.

The collaborative projects in Section II provide exciting cross-curricular learning experiences that reinforce the personal skills and connect together many of the subjects in the national curriculum. Within the six projects there are opportunities to deliver and assess subject content and evaluate essential skills in literacy, numeracy and ICT. Because the activities encourage choice and collaboration, they offer a powerful opportunity to develop independence and to personalise approaches to learning.

The first project in Section II, Bobby's Magic Towers, is an opportunity for learners to review the habits of learning which have been taught explicitly in Section I or through other school provision. However, the projects can be worked through in any order depending on previous experience or existing teaching and curriculum planning needs. As can be seen from the figure below, the intention is that the MAGIC habits in Section I are delivered as the roots that will feed the subject disciplines, the key skills developed are the trunk of the tree and, finally, the principles of assessment for learning – self-assessment, peer review, reflective learning – are used throughout all the projects to shine a nourishing light on the work completed and the learning progress made.

The stories in Section III can be used as an introduction to, or a review of, the habits of emotional intelligence. They can also be used to extend the more able by offering models for writing their own stories about Bobby's adventures. In addition, they can be used as a reminder about the important behaviours we are trying to reinforce.

Project or Section	Essential skills (for more detailed information on national curriculum references please see the individual projects)						National curriculum subject areas					
	Personal and emotional skills	Social skills	Learning and thinking skills	ICT	Numeracy	Literacy	Physical development, health and wellbeing	The arts	History, geography, RS and citizenship	Science and technology	Mathematics	English, communication and languages
Learning Habits Toolkit	X	X	X				X					
Bobby's Magic Towers	X	X	X	X		X	X					
Exodus		X		X		X			X	X	X	
The Wedding Plan	X	X		X	X	X	X	X	X			
Disaster	X	X		X		X			X	X	X	X
International Restaurant		X	X	X		X	X	X	X	X		X
The Time Machine			X	X	X	X			X	X		X
The stories	X	X	X									

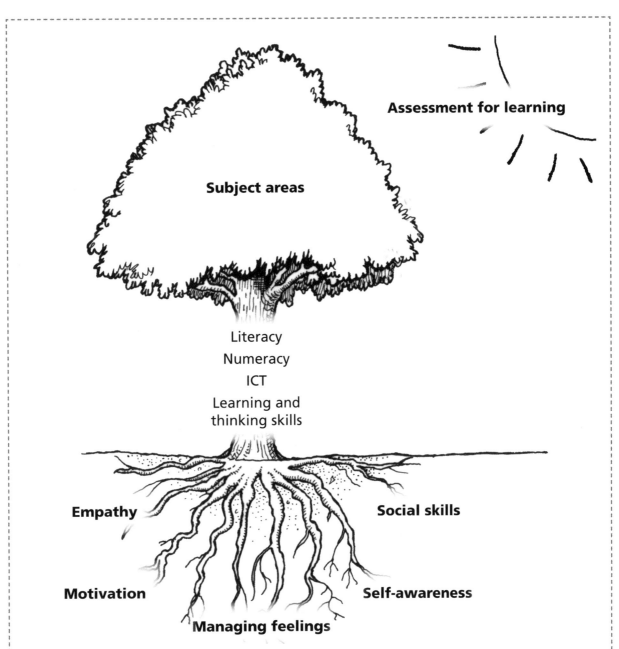

Assessment for learning

Subject areas

Literacy
Numeracy
ICT
Learning and
thinking skills

Empathy

Social skills

Motivation

Self-awareness

Managing feelings

A tentative, evolving curriculum

This book aims to offer learning experiences that are flexible and tentative, reflecting and modelling the learners it wishes to nurture. This learning will create a new teaching that facilitates real learning and hands over some of the control of the learning experiences to the learners. However, the teacher's role is even more important as it guides the embedding of the learning habits through the crucial process of review and reflection on a class and individual level. The planning will be a crucial aspect of this type of learning and the projects may evolve in various different directions. The schemes are not definitive but just a starting point for teachers and children to create amazing, memorable learning experiences. The examples of planning sheets lessons and content are merely the starting point for schools to create their own materials. Within the projects it will be important to measure progress in learning, within lessons and across time. This will ensure the rigour of delivery of subject disciplines as well as evaluate the impact of our teaching. It has been my experience that the progress the pupils will make in this exciting curriculum will amaze us!

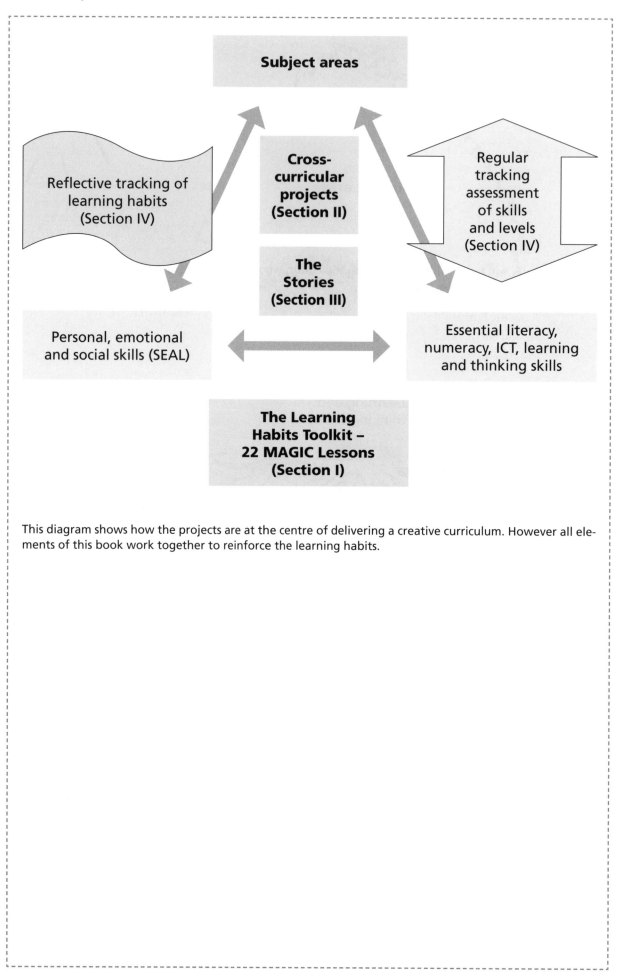

This diagram shows how the projects are at the centre of delivering a creative curriculum. However all elements of this book work together to reinforce the learning habits.

Acknowledgements

I am privileged to meet so many talented teachers who wish to give their students the very best gift you can give a child – a love for learning. They have inspired me to write this book and many of them have tried out some of the activities and added their own genius to create wonderful learning experiences for children. I want thank all those teachers that I have had the chance to work with over the last three years of my roving consultancy – I have learnt so much from them. I also want to thank my colleagues from ITL, particularly Julie, Simon and Will, who are the experts on primary education and who provided so much of the thinking behind this book.

A special thank you to Ian Gilbert, my friend and editor, who always surprises me with his genius and, in this case, patience and encouragement.

I want to thank my husband John for his unconditional support and relentless hard work in helping with the checking and sorting out of my mad thinking. My daughters continue to inspire me as they grow up and demonstrate amazing success and determination in everything they do. This is how I know it works!

I would like to dedicate this book to their father, John Swift, who sadly died in 2008. It was in helping him, in the early days, which encouraged me to learn so much about thinking, and why it matters so much.

Finally, thanks to all those others who encourage and support me in my wonderful life; especially my sister Leslie, my best friend Gill, my friends and neighbours in Tiffield and the very best parents – who taught me everything.

Introduction

What are the learning experiences which will really deliver self-motivated, resilient learners for the 21st century?

In the age of uncertainty...

> *It is not the strongest of the species that survive, nor the most intelligent, but the one most responsive to change.*
>
> **Charles Darwin (1809–1882)**

There is a growing desire globally to discover what we need to change in our education systems to make the difference – the difference between producing young people who simply pass (or fail) exams and creating independent lifelong learners who will not just survive but thrive in the fast moving, knowledge-based economy of the 21st century. Despite prescriptive literacy and numeracy strategies, and constant improvements in performance in formal qualifications, employers complain about a lack of communications skills and of a thirst for learning, aspiration, initiative and self-discipline.

When does this start? Many would argue that children are turned off from learning at younger and younger ages. This book, then, is an attempt to provide learning experiences that not only develop practical and personal skills but also engender a genuine love of learning. It is designed to reflect the aspirations woven through a creative primary curriculum as well as bring together the very successful SEAL (Social and Emotional Aspects of Learning) initiatives together with knowledge of neuroscience, key communication skills and traditional areas of learning. It also encourages a pedagogy that promotes assessment as learning (as opposed to 'of' or 'for') and which promotes metacognition, thinking about thinking, in the classroom.

What is education for?

> *The principal goal of education is to create men who are capable of doing new things, not simply of repeating what other generations have done – men who are creative, inventive and discoverers.*
>
> **Jean Piaget (1896–1980)**
>
> *The purpose of education is to change the thoughts, feelings and actions of students.*
>
> **Benjamin Bloom (1913–1999)**
>
> *Pupils set their own standards and learning objectives, work in teams, assess their own and each others work, solve real world problems. They give their views about what makes a good lesson.*
>
> **Professor David Hargreaves on personalised learning (2006)**

A crucial requirement to deliver these aspirations is to have a greater focus on *how* we learn and a determined drive to develop an educational system that helps children learn effective life skills, something very different from simply learning 'stuff'. (The same 'stuff' that can now be accessed in seconds on the internet anyway.) This paradigm shift in emphasis should also include developing in children an understanding of their own learning profiles and how to use these to raise achievement and develop their potential. This involves teaching children to reflect on how they learn best and how they can develop their flexibility as learners to enable them to transfer skills. For more on this, a good starting point is *Learning Styles in Action* by Barbara Prashnig.

The fundamentals of learning

Teachers, pupils and parents all need to understand how they learn, how to engage the brain and how to manage their minds for learning. Children can then use this knowledge to develop the sorts of 'transferable skills' they can carry with them throughout their lives, regardless of where they go. Skills that will help them become the emotionally intelligent, flexible learners needed for the 21st century workplace.

If we want to deliver this curriculum effectively teachers and learners need to know about about:

■ The power of the brain to 'grow' intelligence

■ Best thinking on learning styles and preferences – and how to develop them

■ How to control thinking and use internal dialogue for motivation

■ The three-part brain – especially the importance of the emotional brain for learning and how a 'reptilian brain state' can create anxiety or anger

■ The importance of goals and deferred gratification

■ The nature of multiple intelligence and how to develop transferable skills

■ Why successful learning behaviours are like habits that we need to practice and whose development we need to take responsibility for throughout life

■ The value of enrichment programmes.

All of the above demonstrate the importance of connecting learning to real life beyond school to create transferable skills and embed the habits of great learning.

Flexible, personalised learning

Collaboration, choice and challenge in the classroom

The style of curriculum that will reinforce the habits of learning, involves pupil-designed learning experiences and collaborative projects that demand negotiation and compromise to achieve outstanding results.

Schools need to develop children's skills in teamwork and cooperation so evident in activities such as sport and theatre. These extra-curricular activities are often simply fitted in outside of – 'extra' – to an overcrowded, content-dominated curriculum. Yet this type of learning is at the centre of a competency-based curriculum which focuses on acquiring skills rather than remembering information. The projects in this book aim to deliver these types of learning experiences whilst learning subject content effectively.

The Primary Curriculum Review

In 2008, Sir Jim Rose was tasked with the job of reviewing what young learners need. This book aims to build on the best recommendations of this Primary Curriculum Review and provide examples of resources that will help you implement a connected, engaging curriculum.

The Primary Review's purpose was to:

■ review the programmes of study and reduce prescription where possible to allow greater flexibility for schools to meet individual pupil's needs and strengths

■ strengthen schools' focus on raising standards in reading, writing and numeracy

■ provide all children with a broad and balanced entitlement to learning, including languages at Key Stage 2

■ make personal development a more central aspect of the primary curriculum

- improve transition and continuity in learning from early years through primary school and then into secondary education.

Sir Jim Rose's final report, delivered in April 2009, proposed the following changes to the primary curriculum to meet these requirements, basing the revised curriculum on three fundamental points:

- reinforcing the importance of literacy, numeracy, information and communication technology (ICT) and learning and thinking skills, personal and emotional skills and social skills as the essentials for learning and life

- reorganising the knowledge, skills and understanding contained in the primary curriculum into six broad areas of learning, and a non-statutory programme of learning for religious education

- creating a less prescriptive curriculum that increases flexibility for personalisation.

With government changes this review has been put to one side and another review may follow, However many schools still wish to pursue a creative curriculum that gives real scope to develop engaging learning experiences that connect together subject disciplines with personal skills for life. Many teachers and leaders welcomed the Rose review outcomes and find they can pursue some of the aims within the present primary curriculum requirements. This book aims to provide resources to build a creative curriculum that develops independent, resilient learners and yet delivers the statutory requirements for subject disciplines and pupil progress.

The digital native jungle rules – why ICT is a key component of the projects

In the global electronic community we now live in, our children have to become more aware of their place in the world and become competent in building rapport with other cultures. It is likely they will work for international companies and be communicating in a virtual environment where geography is no longer a barrier to communication. As the youngsters of the emerging nations, such as China and India, embrace the electronic era with a creativity and determination borne of economic disadvantage, we must ensure that our future generations can compete. Weaving in the use of digital technology, podcasting, blogs, social networking sites and other emerging technologies will be an important evolution of these projects over time. Our youngsters are learning to use laptops and mobile phones before they even arrive at school so it is they who can lead the way when planning the use of technology in their learning experiences.

For example, as part of this process, essential learning skills can be assessed and recorded as an 'e-portfolio' for life. This is an interactive electronic profile which assesses progress, stores evidence, coaches towards improvement and enables the sharing of resources within your school's Virtual Learning Environment. The skills e-portfolio should enable learners to track their progress and build a 'record of achievement' that they can take with them to their secondary school. Their personal tutor can help them record evidence of progress in their skills and their enrichment activities at home and at school, so that these skills become transferable between subjects, home and work.

What type of curriculum will deliver the personal skills?

The models of a compartmentalised curriculum based on subject content, the teacher as an expert and the pupil as a passive recipient, have not produced the skills and competences our young people need to become successful learners. A new, connected, creative curriculum can deliver the skills and habits that help learners take more responsibility for their learning and also personalise it for themselves.

If the above curriculum changes are combined with a rigorous behaviour policy that focuses on choosing to learn (as opposed to being punished for not wanting to learn) and an active pupil voice programme that encourages a sense of ownership, enterprise and responsibility, the possibility of engaging chlidren in a learning culture becomes much more likely.

If we supplement this by teaching the habits of emotional intelligence, habits such as persistence, optimism and self-management, and do this across the curriculum as suggested by the SEAL initiative, then we are achieving the essential shift needed. This applies the research evidence of brain-friendly ways to learn – active participation, variety, challenge and emotional involvement – which combine to make learning exciting but demanding. It's the way we are wired!

A crucial aspect of this new pedagogy is metacognition – essentially reflective practice by both teachers and children. Constant reflection about learning and how and why it works is part of a competency-based curriculum. It is through this reflection that progress is assessed, reviewed and understood.

> *Paul Black and Dylan Wiliam demonstrated the double impact of assessment for learning: it improves scores in national tests and examinations as well as metacognitive skills, including the capacity to learn how to learn. Techniques such as open questioning, sharing learning objectives and success criteria, and focused marking have a powerful effect on the extent to which learners are enabled to take an active role in their learning.*
>
> **John Bransford, Ann Brown and Rodney Cocking, *How People Learn: Brain, Mind, Experience and School* (2000)**

Tracking the development of the personal skills at the lesson level will necessitate implementing the pedagogy that Ofsted requires for 'outstanding' teaching. Setting objectives for 'skills' as well as 'content', will require teachers to build a 'competency focus' into all lessons and projects. This could be achieved by teachers considering a focus for each lesson that attempts to deliver a personal skill as well as the quality of an outcome – and talking about this in the plenary. For example 'You produced a wonderful "time machine". Now, what did you learn about working together?' Or, 'How did you manage your feelings when customers complained in your international restaurant?'. Or 'How are you going to take what you have learnt about leadership and use it in another situation?'

To deliver your new curriculum it may help to consider the following tables.

Embedding	Innovation	Abandon
Curriculum	Competency-based curriculum using cross-curricular projects mapped against essential skills and areas of learning	Separate subject delivery that teaches content out of context
	Encourage the transference of skills across the curriculum through skills audit and the use of competency and content objectives	The compartmentalisation of the curriculum which can restrict the ability to transfer skills and competences to new situations
	Embed communication skills including literacy and numeracy in cross-curricular projects. Use APP (Assessing Pupil Progress) models to assess the skills development	Attempts to manage literacy and numeracy across the curriculum in primary schools with paid posts
	Investigate the International Primary Curriculum and International Baccalaureate for further cross-curricular materials	KS2 coaching for SATs
Timetables	Flexible timetables with longer blocks of time for project or themed work Build in enrichment days or weeks for mixed-age groups	Fixed timetables
Homework	Extended home learning tasks linked to cross-curricular projects For example, learn vocabulary of French food for your international restaurant	Homework as an unrelated extra, driven by a homework timetable
Assessment	Rigorous learner-led assessment for learning through KS1/2 using data available and tracking tools to target underachievers	Summative testing and school league tables
	Develop an e- portfolio of achievements and competences in KS1–3 to include extra-curricular activities and levels of attainment in a variety of subjects with a skills diploma awarded	Bureaucratic assessment models

Preparing learners for the 21st century	Innovation	Abandon
Engaging learners	Establish the ethos and belief in all schools that intelligence can be learnt and that there are a variety of ways to be clever	Notions of fixed and single IQ
	Train teachers to be aware of the optimal environmental conditions for learning: stress-free, praise focused and creatively challenging	Controlling rather than motivating classrooms
	Use of innovative technology such as podcasting, blogs, Twitter feeds, YouTube, digital cameras, mobile phones, video gaming and multimedia applications as part of the demonstration of learning	Limits on aspects of new technology
	Train children to take responsibility for their own learning through an understanding of how to learn and having responsibility for their learning	Children expecting to be entertained and spoon-fed for the exam
	Use assessment for learning and peer-/self-assessment techniques to give learners a true understanding of how to progress	Summative grades that neither motivate nor assist progress in learning
	Create a learning environment that works with the brain in mind and facilitates peripheral learning	Classrooms built for 'chalk and talk' with the teacher as the fount of all knowledge talking at the pupils
	Use novelty, variety, humour, colour, challenge and music – which all appeal to the emotional brain – and have clear, consistent, high expectations to motivate learners	Inconsistent delivery of boring subject content through working from textbooks or copying from the board
	Create positive relationships using a behaviour policy that describes what we want and applies sanctions consistently	The tolerance of bad behaviour that impacts on the learning opportunities for others

Preparing learners for the 21st century	Innovation	Abandon
Pedagogy for outstanding learning	Underpin all lessons with the development of emotional intelligence to include persistence, self-awareness, self-management, optimism and deferred gratification to produce resilient learners	The notion that exists amongst some children (and parents) that they can achieve without determination and hard work
	Reflective learning by teachers and learners leading to regular metacognition	Didactic teaching with pupils spending most of the time listening to the teacher
	Active learning	Focus on copying from textbooks or the board
	Effective teamworking	Teachers 'towing' pupils through the tests and coursework tasks
	Learners able to ask good questions and use sources from the internet effectively	
	Learners designing some of their learning and setting their success criteria	
	Learners talking (on task) more than teachers	
	Philosophical approach through a Community of Enquiry	
	Assessment for learning as a fundamental part of all lessons	
	Language for learning used by teachers and learners	
	Self-motivated learners who can talk about their progress	
	Mistakes seen as learning experience	

Section I
22 MAGIC
Lessons

- Implementing a creative curriculum through cross-curricular projects
- Developing social and emotional intelligence
- Creating independent, confident and lifelong learners

How to use this section

This book is a toolkit for delivering an engaging curriculum for young learners that will develop the habits of emotional intelligence through collaborative activities. The MAGIC lessons offer discrete opportunities for teaching children to understand how they can manage their thinking to develop emotional intelligence and thereby improve their learning. The lessons can be used as a stand-alone course, integrated into the projects or delivered as an introduction to a skills curriculum. The lessons can also be used as one-off classes which may address the needs of certain groups of children.

It is recommended that the MAGIC lessons are delivered prior to the projects as these will help children to understand the concept of developing their competencies, particularly if they haven't had similar input before. Alternatively, these materials can complement any Social and Emotional Aspects of Learning (SEAL) or Learning to Learn provision already delivered at school. The purpose of these lessons is to encourage children to integrate the MAGIC habits into everyday school life to reinforce these behaviours and embed useful learning habits.

The MAGIC habits are outlined below with the lessons that reinforce them referenced. All the habits overlap with each other so each will reinforce the same messages. It will help to make a classroom display of the habits and refer to them throughout the school day. The genie sayings that feature in the lessons are useful to display for peripheral learning (e.g. 'If it's to be, it's up to me'). Bobby's Magic Towers project (on page 127) is an excellent follow-up to these lessons. It reviews the MAGIC habits and encourages learners to create activities that will further develop them.

The stories in Section III can be used at any point to reinforce the messages and encourage real life application of the lessons learnt.

Learning check

Assessment for learning as part of each activity

Each lesson or activity is completed with a learning check plenary where children can reflect on how much progress they have made from the beginning of the lesson. The technique involves considering an arrow that points towards the success criteria and a discussion can take place about:

■ how far the learner thinks they have travelled

■ what has helped them progress

■ what else they need to do to improve and so on.

This reflection can be achieved through self-assessment, peer-assessment or teacher assessment – or a combination of all three.

High expectation is a key factor in great teaching. We always underestimate what our learners can do.

The MAGIC habits	What are they?	Lessons which reinforce a habit
Habit 1 **M** is for motivation	Being able to motivate yourself, even when learning is difficult, is the best habit children can learn at a young age. Understanding yourself and what motivates you involves consideration of beliefs and values and also strategies for managing moods and feelings	1, 2, 3, 4
Habit 2 **A** is for Attitude	This habit is about developing a can-do attitude which includes taking responsibility for learning. It includes the idea of taking positive action rather than feeling like a victim of circumstances. This habit helps children to be more optimistic and independent in a world where watching TV or a computer screen can be their dominant activity. Attitude is about a habitual way of thinking and behaving that can create a positive (or negative) reaction	5, 6, 7, 8, 9
	Negative self-fulfilling prophecies can restrict a child's ambition, particularly when they have learnt this habit at home. For example, Lesson 8 suggests imagining an ambitious future that can become a positive self-fulfilling prophecy	
	These lessons also encourage an open-minded approach to change that promotes flexibility	
Habit 3 **G** is for Gumption	Gumption is about having resourcefulness, courage and common sense. Gaining an awareness of this will certainly help children in their ability to be resilient and determined	10, 11, 12, 13
	The lessons help children to become aware of the need to take risks and push themselves out of their comfort zones	
Habit 4 **I** is for I-learn	'I-learn' is the habit that shows children how to make the most of their brainpower through understanding their learning styles and how the brain reacts to stress	14, 15, 16, 17
Habit 5 **C** is for Communication	Effective communication is an essential skill for future success and these lessons focus on charm and good manners as well as teamwork and body language	18, 19, 20, 21
Review	A review of all habits that take place in the toolkit	22

Teacher's Notes for Lesson 1: Get the MAGIC habits

Learning focus: What are the MAGIC habits for learning?

The aim of this lesson is to make children aware of their unconscious habits and how certain habits can create ways of thinking that help learning.

This session introduces the children to Bobby Brain, who will guide them during their learner's toolkit lessons. He is a miniature brain character and his purpose is to help children realise how clever they can be when they learn how to learn. On the CD-ROM that accompanies this book there are pictures of Bobby that can be downloaded – he can be placed on your classroom wall, onto activity sheets or elsewhere.

The five MAGIC ingredients that make up the habits are outlined and these can be made into a poster with Bobby in the centre. A discussion of what we mean by 'habits' would be worthwhile at this stage. In this book they describe *unconscious behaviours* which can be useful for learning or – equally important – which can act as barriers to learning. Behaviours such as negative self-talk, being easily distracted from the task, intolerance of uncertainty and lack of self-discipline can all become habitual.

Making a MAGIC card is the main activity. This helps give the children a reminder of the habits to keep or take home and share with parents. Some of the children may also have time to make up a poem, song or rap using the MAGIC habit ideas. This can be a group effort and can be performed for the class.

Bobby's own card with his ideas can be drawn on as an example and could be used as part of the classroom display.

Learning check: This is a self-assessment tool to check at the end of each lesson or section how far the children have progressed with their learning. For this lesson it may be possible for the children to be able to tell each other what the MAGIC habits are to show they have met the lesson objective.

Resources needed:

Card to make MAGIC cards

LESSON 1: GET THE MAGIC HABITS

Learning focus: What are the MAGIC habits for learning?

Hi, My name is Bobby Brain.

'Inside my magic lantern are the ingredients that can help you at school and at home. It's taken me a long time and a lot of hard work to become a superhero, flying on my magic carpet around the world, helping children to learn. In this book there are the MAGIC ingredients that will help you become a genius too.

'Sometimes I have been scared or lonely. Sometimes I couldn't be bothered to practise my thinking or even be nice to anyone. But by remembering my magic lantern and listening to my friend the genie's advice I have found out how to make the most of my brain and get on well with everyone.

'If you practise the lessons in this book you will soon start to have all the great habits that will help you learn. We all have bad habits that can get in the way of learning. This book will help you get the good habits which make it easy to learn through your whole life.

'Good luck – and look out for the genie's advice to help you become a great learner.'

If it's to be – it's up to me. This means you can always make a difference.

LESSON 1: GET THE MAGIC HABITS PAGE 2

Learning focus: What are the MAGIC habits for learning?

The five ingredients to make your MAGIC habits are:

1. **M**otivation – This is about understanding what makes *you* happy and want to work hard. Having more of this will make you a great learner and fun to be with too!

2. **A**ttitude – Your attitude is how you think and behave. It is important to have a can-do attitude. This is about *you* taking some action when you need to and having a positive attitude.

3. **G**umption – This is about having resilience, courage and common sense. This is a habit that will give you more strength and energy, especially when things are hard.

4. **I**-learn – This is the habit that helps you find out how you learn best. It will help you use your amazing brain to learn from mistakes and become cleverer.

5. **C**ommunication – This is a very important MAGIC ingredient that will help you make friends and work well in groups.

There are some people that succeed in life and there are others that don't. Scientists now believe there are some special ways of thinking that will decide whether *you* will be a success in life. Bobby Brain is here to help you develop your MAGIC genius.

Remember. It's what you say and how you say it that makes other people feel happy.

LESSON 1: GET THE MAGIC HABITS PAGE 3

Learning focus: What are the MAGIC habits for learning?

UNDERSTANDING THE MAGIC INGREDIENTS

M FOR MOTIVATION

> Football always makes me feel motivated, but when I have to do something I don't like I just tell myself to get on with it. Then I am pleased with the result when it's finished.

A FOR ATTITUDE

> I always try to be positive and in a happy mood because that seems to make things work out well.

G FOR GUMPTION

> Sometimes I need to be brave and work things out for myself. When I moved schools I had to find my way around and make new friends.

i FOR i-LEARN

> I know that I learn best when I listen hard to my teacher then keep trying in different ways to get it right.

C FOR COMMUNICATION

> I always try to make people feel good when I talk to them by listening carefully and smiling.

LESSON 1: GET THE MAGIC HABITS PAGE 4

Learning focus: What are the MAGIC habits for learning?

 ## MAGIC CARDS

Create your own MAGIC card with your own speech bubbles for each of the ingredients: Motivation, Attitude, Gumption, I-learn and Communication.

> I can make myself work hard by telling myself it's worth it.
>
> I motivate myself by thinking of getting a great job.

TIP: Make the card colourful and add pictures. This will help your brain remember the slogans.

Make up a poem, a song or a rap to go with the MAGIC habits. Write the words on your card then sing it to the class.

Learning check ⟶ I know what the MAGIC habits are.

Put yourself on this line to show how close you got to the learning goal.

Teacher's Notes for Lesson 2: What makes you tick?

Learning focus: Know and understand what turns on different feelings in me and how to change my feelings if I need to.

Self-awareness is the first habit required for developing emotional intelligence, so this lesson focuses on how to explore what makes you happy and how to motivate yourself. Understanding emotions and how to control them in yourself and others is crucial to children feeling more powerful and confident. This doesn't mean they will never be unhappy but this lesson aims to help them have a degree of metacognition about it. This means thinking about their thinking and becoming more conscious of how that thinking affects them.

There is lots of evidence to show that the skills that create optimism can be taught. Twenty-one different studies of 10–12 year olds indicated that you can halve the rate of depression and anxiety later in their teens through teaching positive thinking skills (see www.authentichappiness.sas.upenn.edu/Default.aspx).

The starter activity gets the children thinking about emotions. This can become a large collage using pictures or words depending on the age and ability of the children. The paired and class discussion will be highly beneficial here.

The next activity considers ways to change feelings in yourself and others. The discussion should consider how feelings change and how you can alter your feelings. For example, if you are angry and frowning then relax your face, breathe deeply, stand up straight, begin to smile and see how that changes your feelings.

Children can consider what activity can transform them from angry to happy (e.g. playing with a pet, listening to music, hearing a joke, eating chocolate). The habits work on two levels – what you can do and how it affects your mind and body. The purpose here is to get the children to think about feelings and how they are expressed and changed. This activity can also be done using words or pictures depending on the age and ability of the children. Large paper can be used as appropriate.

The self-portrait activity is completed using the hand the pupils don't usually write with. This makes it into a fun activity and not a drawing quality test. The idea is to draw the key different moods that dominate their personality and what it is that creates that mood (e.g. eating dinner with my family for a happy mood).

Reflection on the children's feelings and how they manage them will be an important part of the plenary for this lesson.

The last exercise is about trying explicitly to manage feelings and engage in a positive thinking style. Trying out ways to talk yourself into a good mood would be a great homework activity to attempt for a week.

An extension research activity has been included for homework and discussion at home. It links moods and feelings with beliefs and values.

Resources needed:

Large paper for creating mood changes
Sticky notes
Lots of pictures of faces and different moods

LESSON 2:
WHAT MAKES YOU TICK?

Learning focus: Know and understand what turns on different feelings in me and how to change my feelings if I need to.

The first step to get the MAGIC habits is to know yourself. The aim of this lesson is to help you get to know yourself better. It takes courage to be really honest about yourself – so decide now whether you are brave enough!

 Write down an example or draw a picture of situations when you feel the following:

Angry	Happy	Sad (e.g. When I see animals suffering)	Responsible
Curious	Determined (e.g. When I am playing football I am determined to score a goal)	Scared	Excited

 Discuss these with your neighbour and see if they are similar.

Write down your examples from the angry and happy boxes and put them on a sticky note. Stick them on the board and compare all the answers in the class.

LESSON 2: WHAT MAKES YOU TICK? PAGE 2

Learning focus: Know and understand what turns on different feelings in me and how to change my feelings if I need to.

CHANGING FEELINGS MOOD MAP

Wouldn't it be great if you could change angry to happy or change scared to excited?

On a large sheet of paper choose three moods that don't feel good and draw a face that shows the feeling. Draw wavy lines with arrows that show how you can start in one mood then change it to a different mood.

When you feel angry you stand in particular ways and have a certain expression on your face. Sometimes when you can change this it alters how you feel and helps you feel better.

Draw pictures or write ideas about how you can change your feelings on your lines. Add in some activities that can help you change your mood.

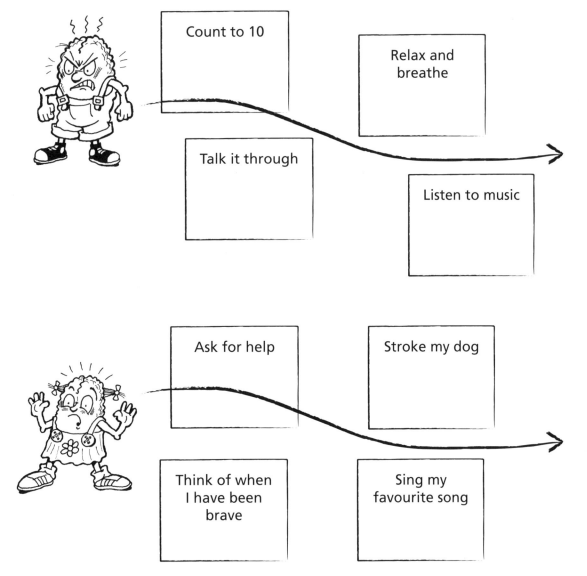

Count to 10

Relax and breathe

Talk it through

Listen to music

Ask for help

Stroke my dog

Think of when I have been brave

Sing my favourite song

LESSON 2:
WHAT MAKES YOU TICK? PAGE 3

Learning focus: Know and understand what turns on different feelings in me and how to change my feelings if I need to.

BOBBY'S BANNER

When we help others it makes us feel good. Write down on this banner three top tips for cheering someone else up.

'Give a compliment and really mean it. Making someone else feel good is the best way to become a confident person.'

What three things have you learned about yourself from this discussion?

1. ....
....

2. ....
....

3. ....
....

If you didn't learn anything that says something about you too! What do you think this could be?

....
....
....
....

LESSON 2: WHAT MAKES YOU TICK? PAGE 4

Learning focus: Know and understand what turns on different feelings in me and how to change my feelings if I need to.

SELF-PORTRAIT

Divide some paper into four sections. With the hand you DON'T usually write with try drawing yourself in your four favourite moods. Make sure your face shows the way you feel. Share these pictures with the class.

GOOD MORNING SUNSHINE!

Think of a positive thing to say to yourself every day when you look in the mirror in the morning. It is the most important thing you will do today! Write it down. Say it aloud. Say it in your head. Louder! Give it a kind, lovely voice. Say it again. Say it every day.

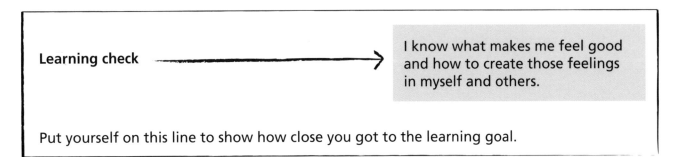

Learning check ⟶ I know what makes me feel good and how to create those feelings in myself and others.

Put yourself on this line to show how close you got to the learning goal.

Teacher's Notes for Lesson 3: What are your beliefs and values?

Learning focus: To understand more about what I believe in and what I value and how it can influence me to be successful.

It is beliefs and values that drive the motivation in all of us. This lesson aims to help learners understand how their beliefs and values can influence their success in positive and negative ways.

The starter helps children to consider what values are and to investigate the link between values and beliefs. The children can create flags that show a symbol and word that represent different values. The class discussion about how these values help them behave in certain ways will be an important aspect of learning. This discussion could also be linked to debates on media messages about body size or material possessions.

Following the discussion, the children can choose their top three values and create a clover leaf display illustrating their values for the class wall. A useful debate about the influence of friends and family on values could help to support and challenge this thinking.

Finally, there are some questions to consider and the children need to decide how their values impact on their answers. The objective is to tease out whether the children really are making decisions based on their values. The essential link between thought and action will lead to certain answers to questions such as 'How would you spend £1,000?'

The final task allows the children to connect the useful values with positive outcomes in education. If they value education (even if their parents don't) it can change their life chances. It is hoped that this lesson will help the children to realise that if they are to be motivated for learning, they need to value it and appreciate that believing school work matters will help them to reach their potential.

The poem written at the end of the lesson to sum up their favourite values will be another good display piece as an outcome for this lesson.

Resources needed:

Paper for writing
Large sugar paper for flags
Coloured pens or paints
Green paper for clover leaves

LESSON 3: WHAT ARE YOUR BELIEFS AND VALUES?

Learning focus: To understand more about what I believe in and what I value and how it can influence me to be successful.

What is most important to you? Put the following things in order. (Remember: the one at the top of the list is the one you value most. Be honest!)

> Friends
> Hobbies
> School work
> Family
> Religion
> Pets
> Appearance
> Money
> World peace

 Discuss with your neighbour why you have chosen to put them in this order. Were there any things you would have liked to add to the list? Write down what they are and where you would put them.

....

....

....

....

....

....

....

....

....

....

....

....

....

LESSON 3: WHAT ARE YOUR BELIEFS AND VALUES? PAGE 2

Learning focus: To understand more about what I believe in and what I value and how it can influence me to be successful.

Values help guide you in how you behave and give you a sense of right and wrong. Here are some top values that people often say are the most important to them: happiness, love, freedom, courage, respect.

FLAG UP YOUR VALUES!

Create a flag for each of these values and discuss what they mean in the way you might live your life.

Beliefs help you develop your values. How do the beliefs you have affect your values?

Belief	Value
I believe school work is good for me and I should always do my best	Education
I believe that I should always be loyal to my friends	Friendship and trust
I believe that we should be polite and consider each other's feelings	Respect

Learning focus: To understand more about what I believe in and what I value and how it can influence me to be successful.

Write down some more beliefs and how they may become values. Where do your beliefs come from? Which values will make you happy at school?

....

....

....

....

....

....

....

....

....

'I believe the more I learn the more brave I become and I know it's only me that can really make me work hard. That's why my three values are learning, courage and responsibility.'

Decide what your top three values are:

My top three values

LESSON 3: WHAT ARE YOUR BELIEFS AND VALUES? PAGE 4

Learning focus: To understand more about what I believe in and what I value and how it can influence me to be successful.

Draw a clover leaf and write your three values – one on each leaf. Draw a picture to go with each value.

The Primary Learner's Toolkit © Jackie Beere and Crown House Publishing Ltd, 2010

LESSON 3: WHAT ARE YOUR BELIEFS AND VALUES? PAGE 5

Learning focus: To understand more about what I believe in and what I value and how it can influence me to be successful.

Try doing these tasks:

1. Write down three things you believe are important for anyone to be happy.

   (1) .... (2) .... (3) ....

2. If you won £1,000, what would you spend it on?

   ....

3. What makes a good friend?

   ....

4. What do you want to be doing when you are 30 years old?

   ....

How do your values affect your answers?

....

What values will help you be successful at school?

....

What values will help you be motivated when you find things hard?

....

Write a short poem about these values to inspire you when you need it.

....

....

....

....

Learning check ⟶ I know what my values are and how they can help me at school.

Put yourself on this line to show how close you got to the learning goal.

Teacher's Notes for Lesson 4: Managing your mood

Learning focus: To know how to manage my moods to help me get motivated.

The aim of this lesson is to help children understand their own state of mind and how to manage their moods in positive ways, and also to understand the influence they can have on the moods of others.

Helping children consider why toddlers have tantrums and how adults can do the same will highlight the reasons why we lose control of our emotions. Controlling our emotions is at the core of this lesson and the first step for children is to be able to talk openly about emotions. There are many supplementary materials provided in the Social and Emotional Aspects of Learning (SEAL) programme (available at www.teachernet.co.uk).

The connection between mind and body is explored in this lesson. It is a good time to make the whole class fake some laughter for a few minutes and see if it makes them feel differently. When we laugh, our brain chemistry changes – even if it is fake!

The power of compliments – given and taken – to make us feel good about ourselves are discussed in the next activity.

At the other end of the scale, children need to understand that stress can work to give us focus, energy and courage, as well as being a negative force if it is not managed properly. The story offers an opportunity to put these ideas into a narrative. Pictures can be used to show moods if this better suits the ability of the class.

The last part of the lesson involves creating a business card with a picture, name and slogan on it that could help improve mood just by looking at it or holding it.

The extension task is to make a 'mood monitor' that can be pinned on their bedroom wall and help children become more aware of their own mood.

Resources needed:

Pictures of people demonstrating various moods
Paper
Stiff card for making a business card, plus some examples showing design logos etc.

LESSON 4: MANAGING YOUR MOOD

What mood are you in today?

Learning focus: To know how to manage my moods to help me get motivated.

MOOD CONTROL

Can you put yourself in a good or bad mood? How?

Tell each other a story about a toddler having a tantrum. What is the best way to handle a small child having a tantrum? Write three pieces of advice you would give to a parent.

1. ....

2. ....

3. ....

What puts you in a good mood? What puts you in a bad mood?

Good mood	Bad mood
Playing a computer game	When I am hungry

LESSON 4: MANAGING YOUR MOOD PAGE 2

Learning focus: To know how to manage my moods to help me get motivated.

Your face and your posture are very influenced by your mood. Can they influence how you feel? Try smiling when you feel grumpy.

Laugh loudly NOW. Just by laughing endorphins (natural chemicals in your brain linked to pleasure) are triggered that make you feel good.

'When you stand up straight with your head up and a smile on your face it is impossible to be in a bad mood! Try it!'

MOOD CONTROL TASK

Think of five ways to put yourself in a good mood.

1. ....

2. ....

3. ....

4. ....

5. ....

Think of five ways to put your friend in a good mood.

1. ....

2. ....

3. ....

4. ....

5. ....

LESSON 4: MANAGING YOUR MOOD PAGE 3

Learning focus: To know how to manage my moods to help me get motivated.

Think of five ways to put your mum or another member of your family in a good mood.

1. ....

2. ....

3. ....

4. ....

5. ....

How can you get into the habit of being in such a good mood?

....

....

....

....

On a separate piece of paper write a story about someone who wakes up every morning and is in such a good mood that she or he then spreads it to everyone during the day.

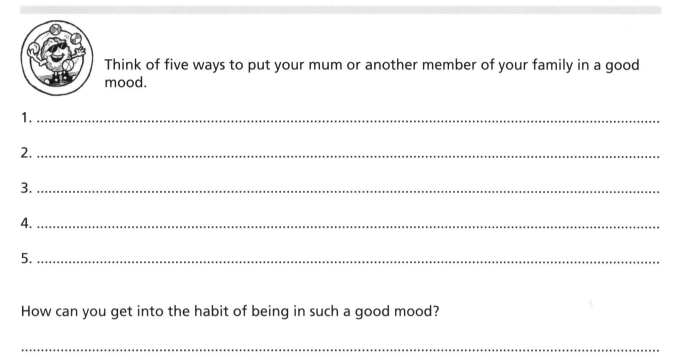

'Good moods are infectious – so spread something good. I imagine a pretend happiness spray that I can spray over miserable people to make them laugh. I can also do the same by saying something nice to them – something that is true and honest but makes them feel good. Try it – say something nice to someone today and watch them glow!'

LESSON 4: MANAGING YOUR MOOD PAGE 4

Learning focus: To know how to manage my moods to help me get motivated.

 Have you noticed that the more you *think* about being in a good mood and happy, the more you *feel* it? Why is that?

Can stress help? List three ways that stress can help us sometimes.

1. ....

2. ....

3. ....

Do we need bad moods sometimes? Why?

....

....

....

....

....

....

....

ACTIVITY: CREATE YOUR OWN MOOD CARD

Create a business card that helps to remind you to feel in a good mood. Include a logo or picture, a slogan and your name in beautiful letters.

Learning check ————————————➔ I know how to understand my mood and how to change it if I need to.

Put yourself on this line to show how close you got to the learning goal.

Talk to your family about moods and pass on some of Bobby's tips!

Teacher's Notes for Lesson 5:
Have a can-do attitude

Learning focus: To know that I can take action and make things happen for myself by having a positive attitude.

The aim of this lesson is to reflect on how children can make things happen for themselves by having a positive attitude rather than being a victim of events. This is quite a challenge as children are so often the powerless victims of experiences such as divorce or illness. However, the attitude they adopt is often the key to creating a response that will lead to a more positive outcome.

The more we can encourage children to be aware of their thinking, the more they can develop a philosophical approach that will prepare them for the traumas of adolescence. We want to help them to develop strategies for coping with the various events that life may bring to them. Many children get this training from parents and families, but some do not, so at school we can raise awareness by teaching strategies directly. Many children get into the habit of not taking responsibility for their learning during Key Stages 2 and 3, so the primary aim of this lesson is to make them feel they can be great learners and that this is, to some extent at least, within their control.

There is some evidence to show that even thinking the words 'I can!' has a positive impact on brain chemistry and makes us stronger. Developing a habit of this type of thinking creates an optimistic attitude that will benefit children in all areas of their lives.

Bobby's input is a fun activity to create a dance called the 'Can-Can' which will help children relate to this outlook.

The example given of a disabled artist leads to further research on stories about the heroic lives of individuals who were born with disabilities but turned their lives into something special.

The roleplay activity will engage children in the way we can 'reframe' a situation by changing our reaction to events.

For the learning check at the end, the children could swap the sayings they have written and learn them by heart.

Resources needed:

IT for research
Writing book or paper

LESSON 5: HAVE A CAN-DO ATTITUDE

If it's to be it's up to me.

Learning focus: To know that I can take action and make things happen for myself by having a positive attitude.

'Sometimes we think someone else should do things for us – or maybe we should do what our friends say – even when it doesn't feel right. Often it's good to think about how we react to things that happen and take our own action instead of blaming others and making excuses. Have a can-do attitude!'

There is only one person who is responsible for your happiness – that person is you.

I CAN ...

Complete twenty or more sentences that start with 'I can …'

I can ....

I can ....

I can ....

I can ....

I can ....

I can ....

I can ....

I can ....

I can ....

I can ....

I can ....

I can ....

I can ....

I can ....

LESSON 5: HAVE A CAN-DO ATTITUDE PAGE 2

Learning focus: To know that I can take action and make things happen for myself by having a positive attitude.

I can ....

I can ....

I can ....

I can ....

I can ....

Think of three 'I can'ts' and convert them into 'I cans' (e.g. I can't fly an aeroplane – yet. But I can fly *in* an aeroplane!).

I can't ....

I can't ....

I can't ....

'When you think "I can" your brain gets motivated, so ban "I can't" and say "I can" as much as possible!'

There is a dance called the Can-Can, which Bobby thinks has got a very happy, catchy tune. Find out about and show your friends how to do it. When you think about it or remember the tune also remember that 'can-can' thoughts make you more motivated.

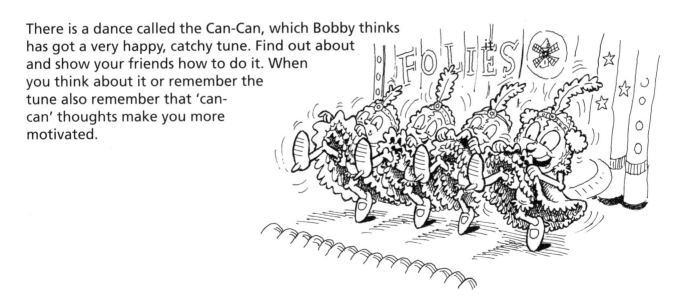

LESSON 5:
HAVE A CAN-DO ATTITUDE PAGE 3

Learning focus: To know that I can take action and make things happen
for myself by having a positive attitude.

CAN YOU MAKE A HAPPY LIFE FOR YOURSELF EVEN IF SAD THINGS HAPPEN TO YOU?

There is a true story about a girl who was born with no arms and no legs because her mother took a drug to control morning sickness when she was pregnant. Despite this, the girl became a famous artist and sculptor, campaigning for the rights of the disabled and was immortalised by a statue in Trafalgar Square.

On the same day a beautiful, healthy baby boy was born into a wealthy, caring family. The boy went to the best schools but had a bad attitude and didn't want to learn. He joined a gang in his teenage years and got into trouble with the police. He was in prison by the time he was 25, leaving his family grieving at his wasted life.

Group discussion: How could this boy have changed things? Why do some people have everything and lose it? Why do some people have bad problems and make the best of it?

ACTIVITY: A STORY OF COURAGE AND DETERMINATION

Think of some examples of how people have turned tragedy into triumph.

....

....

....

Research the story of one of our Paralympics champions and share it with the class.

What are the qualities you admire in these athletes?

....

How can you get more of these qualities?

....

....

Learning focus: To know that I can take action and make things happen for myself by having a positive attitude.

'99% of all failures come from people who have a habit of making excuses.'

George Washington Carver (1864–1943)

Bobby's MAGIC formula:

Stuff happens + you act = outcome

Give up all your excuses and take 100% responsibility for your life!

The only thing you can change when 'stuff happens' is your reaction to it. The stuff has happened! Now, how will you deal with it?

Dealing with it can include how you first *think* about it and especially your attitude. Are you positive or negative?

Try it next time something happens. Change your reaction and see if it changes the outcome.

'Your attitude is the way you behave, what you say and what you do – it matters. Having a positive attitude can make even the most difficult problem easier. Have you got a positive attitude?'

LESSON 5: HAVE A CAN-DO ATTITUDE PAGE 5

Learning focus: To know that I can take action and make things happen for myself by having a positive attitude.

ROLEPLAY

Act out these scenes in two different ways that show a different reaction:

• You are playing around in the house on a rainy day and break something valuable.

• You are starving and dinner is served but it is food you hate.

• You want to go out with your friends but it is getting late and you have homework to do.

'Be prepared to change ... if you always do what you have always done – you'll always get what you always got.'

Think of two sayings that will help you take action that will result in a positive outcome.

1. ....

....

....

2. ....

....

....

| Learning check ⟶ | I know how to have a positive attitude that makes good things happen for me. |

Put yourself on this line to show how close you got to the learning goal.

Teacher's Notes for Lesson 6: Going for goals

Learning focus: I know how to set myself ambitious goals and targets that will help me take action and feel positive.

The aim of this lesson is to focus on the power of goals to motivate. There is lots of evidence to suggest that thinking ahead and planning for goals is a powerful force for learning. It doesn't matter if the goals are more like dreams – but children may need help getting beyond football or *X Factor* ambitions!

Outliers by Malcolm Gladwell offers inspirational accounts of how genius is developed through many long hours of hard work and practice (10,000 hours to be precise). Hence the purpose of this lesson: to make children realise that hard work and practice are essential for reaching any goal.

Considering role models and how they have achieved their dream goals will provide lots of interesting activities and could be developed into a full project.

The MAGIC goal maker helps the children develop ways of thinking that unpick the route to their goal and emphasise their part in the plan.

The planning of short term and long term goals is an important process to go through and an excellent habit to get into. These exercises can be done using pictures or words depending on the ability of the children.

Finally, the activity that looks forward to when they are 30 years old will help children develop a sense of their future and how their motivation now could impact on their goals then.

The winding path could also show stages along the way, and for older children the signposts, bridges, ditches and so on really help them to work out what may lie ahead in their school and work career. For younger children they may want to think about their school life.

The learning check could involve children giving an example of how they will set goals and then sharing these with the class.

Resources needed:

Picture or videos of heroes
Writing paper/book
Large sheets of paper for winding path to the future activity

LESSON 6: GOING FOR GOALS

Learning focus: I know how to set myself ambitious goals and targets that will help me take action and feel positive.

'My goal is to be a great teacher who helps lots of children all over the world become better learners. I decided to make this my goal quite a long time ago and I think it is coming true. It has taken me about 10,000 hours of hard work and practice to learn enough about the brain to write this book. I also want to learn to play the piano one day ... and speak a foreign language ... and play tennis ... It's great having goals. It gives me a positive attitude to everything! The most powerful habit for success is setting yourself goals and ... believing you can achieve them.'

HOW DID THEY DO IT?

Think of three people you admire:

1. ....

2. ....

3. ....

All in the mind ...
Nobody believed that anyone could run the 4-minute mile. It was said to be physically impossible. Roger Bannister succeeded where others had failed. The next year, 37 more runners broke the record. How did Roger Bannister achieve the impossible?

What were their goals? How did they achieve them?

....

....

....

Successful people have these things in common:

1. They had a goal or a dream.

2. They believed they could achieve it.

3. They used MAGIC habits that worked to achieve their goals.

If they can do it – *you* can. First you have to set yourself short term and long term goals and think about how you will set about achieving them.

LESSON 6:
GOING FOR GOALS PAGE 2

Learning focus: I know how to set myself ambitious goals and targets that will help me take action and feel positive.

Fill in a MAGIC goal maker like the one below. Look at the example Bobby has filled in for you and write down your own long term goal.

MAGIC goal maker
Think of a goal (don't forget to aim high!). *I want to be a pilot.*
How could you make it happen? *Work well at school and get good qualifications.* *Find out what extra things I could do outside school to make me a good pilot.*
What can you do today to make it more likely to come true? *Join the Air Cadets.* *Talk to someone who knows about this job to get the top tips for what I need.*
How can you remind yourself about this goal? *Put a picture of an aeroplane on my wall and stick a photo of me in the cockpit!* *Try to visit the pilot's cockpit next time I fly in an aeroplane.*

LESSON 6:
GOING FOR GOALS PAGE 3

Learning focus: I know how to set myself ambitious goals and targets that will help me take action and feel positive.

MAGIC goal maker
Think of a goal (don't forget to aim high!). ....
How could you make it happen? ....
What can you do today to make it more likely to come true? ....
How can you remind yourself about this goal? ....

LESSON 6: GOING FOR GOALS PAGE 4

Learning focus: I know how to set myself ambitious goals and targets that will help me take action and feel positive.

The time to start working towards your goals is *now*. Simply by writing down a goal you make your own motivation start working for you.

Now think about this week and create three important goals:

1. ....
....
2. ....
....
3. ....
....

Create two goals for the next year:

1. ....
....
2. ....
....

Write a paragraph or fill in the pathway describing your life as you would like it to be when you are 30 years old. Remember to say how you got there.

....

....

....

....

LESSON 6: GOING FOR GOALS PAGE 5

Learning focus: I know how to set myself ambitious goals and targets that will help me take action and feel positive.

TASK: SEARCHING FOR YOUR HERO

At home, research into the lives of one of your heroes. Find out three things they did to achieve their success and write them down.

1. ....
....

2. ....
....

3. ....
....

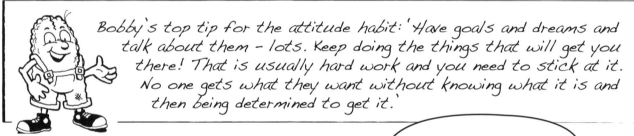

Bobby's top tip for the attitude habit: 'Have goals and dreams and talk about them – lots. Keep doing the things that will get you there! That is usually hard work and you need to stick at it. No one gets what they want without knowing what it is and then being determined to get it.'

If you can dream it, you can do it.

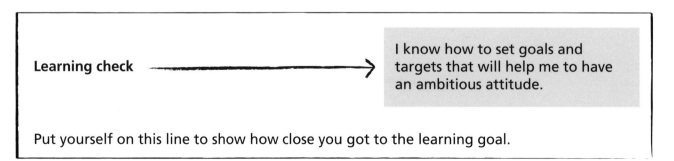

Learning check ⟶ I know how to set goals and targets that will help me to have an ambitious attitude.

Put yourself on this line to show how close you got to the learning goal.

Teacher's Notes for Lesson 7: Developing optimism

Learning focus: To know what we mean by optimism and how to get it.

This lesson aims explicitly to develop optimism as a learned skill that becomes a habit. There is plenty of evidence to show that this can be done and that it will make a difference to learning outcomes and the ability to be successful and happy (Seligman 2002).

We all have horrible thoughts and imagine catastrophic outcomes but the purpose of optimism is to challenge this thinking – habitually. The optimism needs to be realistic too: difficult things do happen. However, children can still be in control of how they react by having a positive response and building on it.

It is important to discuss the point of view that says we can use pessimism to protect ourselves from negative outcomes. If we expect the worst and we are proved right, it may feel better but it doesn't change the outcome. However, nurturing hope will be beneficial for many children. We can also take this opportunity to talk about how we cope with disappointment when things don't turn out well.

The reframing exercise sets up methods for challenging thoughts of disaster and trying to see positive consequences. Seligman talks of using 'signature strengths' to address challenges and the next exercise builds on this idea. The children take a large piece of paper and draw their signature on it with a thick crayon or paintbrush as in an abstract painting. Pupils can then decorate it by writing in their strengths around the signature. These qualities (e.g. musical, sporty, loyal) will help them develop their optimism in ways that are realistic.

The optimism pie encourages children to consider what the whole recipe might be for the pie – including the cooking method, such as stirring, heating up or freezing – there are no rules!

Finally, the rainbow aims to get children to create a list of the positive things in their lives that they can pin on their wall at home to remind them to count their blessings.

A good plenary would be a game where you give them a moan and they have to reframe it laced with optimism.

Resources needed:

Paper
Coloured pens or paints for creating the rainbow

LESSON 7: DEVELOPING OPTIMISM

Learning focus: To know what we mean by optimism and how to get it.

'I always look on the bright side because there is usually a good side to everything. If there isn't then I try to think about it in a good way. When I get something wrong I can think that at least I got parts of it right and that I tried. When it's raining I can think at least I'm indoors and we won't be having a drought like in Africa. If I lose some money I try to accept that someone else might enjoy finding it!

'My challenge to you is to find your optimistic streak and paint the town with it! There is always a silver lining to every cloud!

'Being positive in a practical way means finding good sensible solutions and positive ways of looking at things.'

It's still half full!

TURN PESSIMISM INTO OPTIMISM

Optimism is all about seeing the positive side of a situation – and making this a habit. Think of things that seem difficult and show how you can turn around the thinking.

What's the worst thing that can happen?	Make it half full
e.g. You break your arm falling off your bike	You get lots of sympathy, possibly a rest in front of the TV and get some great signatures on your plaster!

LESSON 7: DEVELOPING OPTIMISM PAGE 2

Learning focus: To know what we mean by optimism and how to get it.

What strengths have *you* got that will help you turn negative into positive?

....

....

....

....

....

MY SIGNATURE STRENGTHS FOR OPTIMISM

On a huge piece of paper draw your signature as wild and wacky as you like. Now write and draw pictures of the things you are good at in and around your name.

Here is Bobby's:

LESSON 7: DEVELOPING OPTIMISM PAGE 3

Learning focus: To know what we mean by optimism and how to get it.

MAKE AN OPTIMISM PIE

What might go in an optimism pie? Things that make you feel good? Here are some possible ingredients. Add some of your own and draw the pie.

Ingredients:

5 sheets of sunshine

2 good friends

2 positive sayings

3 good ideas

1 game of football

Mix up with some chocolate sauce and bake for ten minutes.

LESSON 7: DEVELOPING OPTIMISM PAGE 4

Learning focus: To know what we mean by optimism and how to get it.

RAINBOW

Draw a rainbow and write all the great things in your life onto it. Pin this on your bedroom wall and look at it every day.

The genie has sayings to keep up your optimism levels:

'It could be much worse.'

'I can learn something from this.'

'If it doesn't kill me it makes me stronger.'

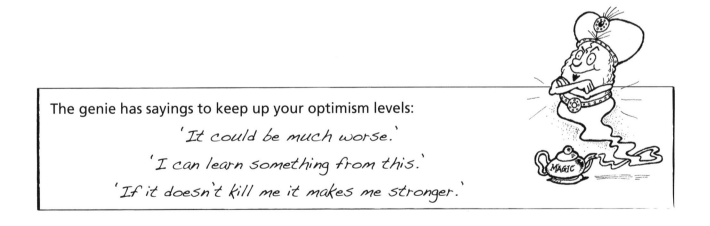

Learning check ——————————————➔ I know what optimism is and how to think in a positive way when I need to.

Put yourself on this line to show how close you got to the learning goal.

Teacher's Notes for Lesson 8: Mind power

Learning focus: To know how to think in ways that develop a positive view of the future.

The aim of this lesson is to introduce the children to the idea of self-belief as a tool for developing self-fulfilling prophecies that create an optimistic view of life.

The lesson starts with a fun look at the various ways people predict their own futures and whether it works. Telepathy, clairvoyance and miracles could be discussed, if appropriate.

The discussion should centre on the impact of hearing a story about your future and believing it. Does this change the outcome? The story of *Macbeth* is the ultimate example of this, so if it is appropriate to read or watch some of the play this may be an extra opportunity for extension work.

The timeline activity gives the children a chance to start predicting their own future and link back to the goal-setting (Lesson 6).

Playing some songs that inspire you as their teacher and giving the children your inspiring motto will encourage them to think about their own inspiring songs and help them to create their own saying. Talk about what advice you would give your 15-year-old self, if you could, looking back. Now ask the children to write a letter to themselves when they are 15 – looking forward. After these have been shared they can be put away somewhere safe to read at age 15. (There are excellent examples of this in Joseph Galliano's book *Dear Me* where celebrities have written letters to their 16-year-old selves.)

The final exercise is about making mind movies. This takes the children through the technique of visualisation to help them practice creating positive images of the future. Make sure they use VAK (visual, auditory, kinaesthetic) techniques during the process as this makes it much more powerful. Some children will find it hard to see the pictures in their head but they may be able to feel or hear aspects of their future success.

The learning check aims to ensure children have imagined their future success and appreciate how it can help to create positive self-fulfilling prophecies.

Resources needed:

Examples of horoscopes or a crystal ball
Examples of inspirational music (e.g. 'Search for the Hero Inside Yourself' by M People or 'I Believe I Can Fly' by R Kelly)
Relaxing instrumental music for visualisation exercise

LESSON 8: MIND POWER

Learning focus: To know how to think in ways that develop a positive view of the future.

Mind power means creating your own magic. Self-belief means creating your own future. So how powerful is your mind? Can you *make* things happen?

What do you know about:

- Telepathy
- Fortune telling
- Astrology.

A Scottish story

Macbeth is a play written by William Shakespeare about a talented and successful Scottish soldier who met some witches who told him a story. They told him he was going to be King of Scotland. It was an exciting and wonderful ambition for Macbeth.
This prediction made him think and consider how he could make it come true. He told his wife and she encouraged him to believe he deserved to be king and to find a way to make it happen. In the end, Macbeth decided to make it happen by killing Duncan, the King of Scotland, who was his friend. So Macbeth did become King of Scotland but he never recovered from the guilt of killing his friend to make the prediction come true.

Macbeth made this prediction come true in an evil way. Could it have come true anyway? Can predictions sometimes have bad effects?

- How does it affect you if someone tells you that you *will* pass a test?

  ....

  ....

- Can anyone see into the future?

  ....

  ....

- With a partner list positive and negative points about fortune telling.

  ....

  ....

  ....

  ....

  ....

  ....

LESSON 8:
MIND POWER PAGE 2

Learning focus: To know how to think in ways that develop a positive view of the future.

CREATE A TIMELINE

For many thousands of years human beings have been trying to predict their future without success.

However, there is a way to predict your future – by planting seeds of positive thoughts that then grow and become reality. Make a timeline that ends fifteen years from now. Draw it on a big piece of paper. Predict lots of great things for yourself and mark them on your line. Maybe you will have a marriage, a house and family, as well as several careers on your timeline. Have some fun and be really ambitious. You can write and draw pictures of your own future!

PRACTISE THE HABITS

Some of the habits we have been learning about need to be practised to make them work to predict your great future:

- Set goals – big ambitious ones that you put up on the wall in your bedroom.
- Create positive mental pictures of your life at school and at home and think about them for several minutes each day.
- See mistakes as learning experiences.
- Be good to others – give out compliments and kindnesses. They will come back to you eventually.
- See yourself as a good learner.
- Say positive things to yourself – don't let *you* put *you* down.
- Praise your own and other people's success.

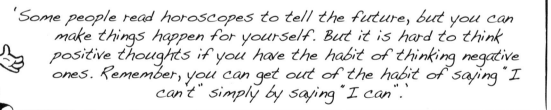

'Some people read horoscopes to tell the future, but you can make things happen for yourself. But it is hard to think positive thoughts if you have the habit of thinking negative ones. Remember, you can get out of the habit of saying "I can't" simply by saying "I can".'

DEAR ME ...

Write a letter to yourself when you are 15 years old. Give advice and encouragement to your teenage self. Share your letter with the class. Put it in an envelope and hide it somewhere until you are 15.

LESSON 8: MIND POWER PAGE 3

Learning focus: To know how to think in ways that develop a positive view of the future.

'There are ways to help you remember to be optimistic and create a good future for yourself: music is MAGIC. Having a song that makes you feel happy, confident and inspired can help. Think of one now.

'Have a slogan that will help to motivate you. Here are some of mine: "I believe I can fly", "The harder I work the luckier I get".'

> If you think you can, or if you think you can't, you're right.

MIND MOVIES

Remember a time when you had a big success. If you can't think of a time, simply make one up! Now make a movie in your mind of that successful time. Get the picture clear and cinema-sized in your head. Turn up the colour and the sound and the size of the picture. Remember what it felt like to be that great success. See what you could see and hear what you could hear as everyone complimented you. Keep that feeling going for a few moments and then think about a song that makes you feel great to go with the images you have. Put it onto your success movie soundtrack with mega-surround sound. Create a slogan to go with all these positive feelings – something like 'I can do it' or 'Go for it'. Say it loud in your head so that you link – or 'anchor' – all those feelings with the slogan. Add a gesture to support it – a thumbs-up or victory sign perhaps.

'If you see it, hear it and act it then you will feel it. By imagining success you will make it more likely to happen. Try this whenever you need lots of courage or energy.'

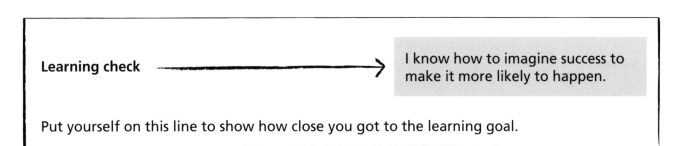

Learning check ⟶ I know how to imagine success to make it more likely to happen.

Put yourself on this line to show how close you got to the learning goal.

Teacher's Notes for Lesson 9: Open to adventure

Learning focus: To know how to be brave about trying new things.

The aim of this lesson is to expand the 'comfort zone' of the children and make them more willing to try new things and take risks in learning.

Children often develop habits that prevent them from attempting new things. However the fewer novel experiences they have, the more they will be fearful. This lesson aims to encourage them to understand why they are frightened and find strategies to overcome their fear. Drawing the two circles and thinking about what they are comfortable with in learning, and what makes them afraid, aims to identify the causes of fearful feelings and then help to argue against them.

The next exercise explores other fears and whether they are rational or not. Examining the thinking that goes on when you decide you don't want to pick up a spider makes you think about the possible catastrophic consequences and then challenge them. What would motivate you to pick up a spider? Money? Presents? What about if it would save your life if you did? How can you then make yourself brave enough to do it? That is the nub of the lesson. How can I say things to myself that will help me be open to new things and brave enough to try things that don't feel comfortable?

The other activities help children practise strategies to develop the courage to do things that are challenging. Finally, children can work in teams to create a programme called 'I'm a Learner … Get Me Out of Here!' which challenges them to take part in activities outside their comfort zones. This could be facing a fear of spiders or public singing. The Bushtucker Trials (from *I'm a Celebrity … Get Me Out of Here*), where celebrities earn stars for overcoming their fears, may be familiar to children.

The learning check could involve doing something brave to demonstrate how they have progressed, such as singing a song in front of the class.

Resources needed:

Large paper for circles exercise
Large paper for planning the 'I'm a Learner …' programme

LESSON 9: OPEN TO ADVENTURE

Learning focus: To know how to be brave about trying new things.

If you are open to new ideas every mistake can become a learning experience.

CHALLENGING YOUR COMFORT ZONES

Draw two circles. Put all the things that are easy for you to do inside the inner circle (e.g. go to football practice, sing in the bath).

Put things in the outer circle that you would like to do, but can't do yet (e.g. play well enough to be in the school football team, sing a solo in assembly).

LESSON 9: OPEN TO ADVENTURE PAGE 2

Learning focus: To know how to be brave about trying new things.

What can you do now?

	Would do	Might do	Never do
Talk to someone in school who I don't know at playtime			
Sing on my own in assembly			
Have a garage sale to sell all my old toys for charity			
Eat a snail			
Cook dinner for the family			
Give up television			
Speak up against a group if I disagree			
Go skydiving			

Take your 'never do' list and write bubbles like the one below that show what you think.

I'm scared ...
I don't like it ...

LESSON 9:
OPEN TO ADVENTURE PAGE 3

Learning focus: To know how to be brave about trying new things.

Now think of five more things that you would find difficult to do and discuss with your neighbour or a small group what would make you do them.

1. ....

2. ....

3. ....

4. ....

5. ....

 'Sometimes you can get scared of a thought. If I think about spiders crawling up my arm, it's scary and I don't want to do it but if I had to pick up a spider because it would help someone else who was more scared – I would do it! I can train my brain to think differently about the spider. I could keep calm, get a jar and pick it up safely. I would be proud to be so brave!'

WHAT ARE YOU SCARED OF?

The FEAR factor: **F**alse **E**xperiences **A**ppearing **R**eal. What presses your panic buttons?

What happens to your body when you are scared?

What is claustrophobia?

Discuss in a group what other phobias you know about.

Why do people get phobias?

How can they overcome them?

LESSON 9:
OPEN TO ADVENTURE PAGE 4

Learning focus: To know how to be brave about trying new things.

HOW TO HAVE COURAGE

Choose something from the outside circle that you would like to do. Take control of your thinking and what you say to yourself in your head. For example 'Keep calm, relax, you can do it' instead of 'I can't want to do this!' Give yourself motivation – you have to want to do it. Imagine yourself doing it – and loving it. Visualise how you will feel when you have done it.

The more you push yourself out of your comfort zone the stronger and braver you will become.

CHALLENGE (THIS WILL TAKE COURAGE!)

Stand up and explain to the class what courageous thing you would like to do and why. Describe doing it in the present tense (not '*I would like* to sing in front of the class' but '*I like* to sing in front of the class') for a couple of sentences.

Why should you challenge yourself to do things that are hard and different?

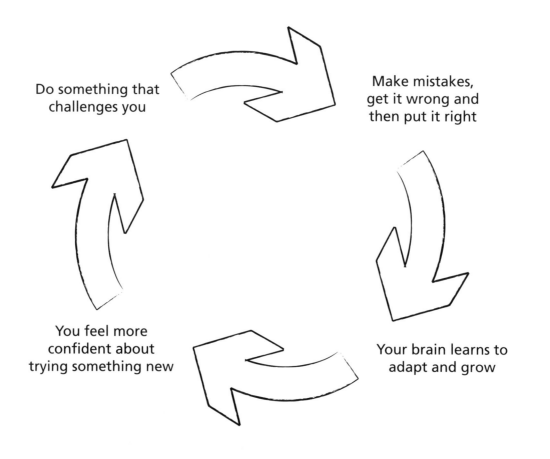

Do something that challenges you

Make mistakes, get it wrong and then put it right

Your brain learns to adapt and grow

You feel more confident about trying something new

LESSON 9:
OPEN TO ADVENTURE PAGE 5

Learning focus: To know how to be brave about trying new things.

I'M A LEARNER ... GET ME OUT OF HERE

Create a TV programme to help build up courage and an open-minded approach. How can you help people to try new things they have never done before? Will you offer rewards or punishments? The camp should have all sorts of challenges for children – physical, emotional and intellectual. It could be eating different foods, holding a worm or playing a computer game – but it must be a personal challenge. Now design publicity material that is meant to convince others to come to the camp.

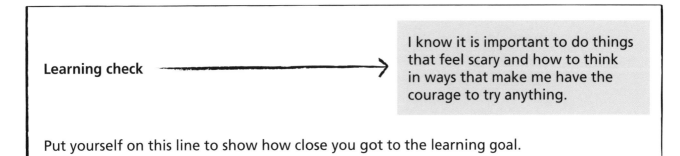

Learning check ⟶ I know it is important to do things that feel scary and how to think in ways that make me have the courage to try anything.

Put yourself on this line to show how close you got to the learning goal.

Teacher's Notes for Lesson 10: Getting more gumption

Learning focus: To know how to develop your gumption and stick at things even when it gets tough.

The aim of this lesson is to develop the resilient thinking that represents gumption. This will help children be more persistent and determined in their learning.

The notion of 'gumption' has been selected as it may be a new word for children and has a certain appeal in its traditional sense of character building qualities. The activities reflect on what we mean by gumption and lead to creating a gumption tree for the classroom. They also develop an understanding of how we can all grow our own gumption by what we do and say. There are links with the film *Forrest Gump* which could be shown in parts to demonstrate what can be achieved through courage, determination and by simply keeping on keeping on.

Ideas are suggested in the lesson plan about putting emotions on the roots of the tree and useful sayings on the branches. This could also lead to adding digital photos of the children themselves showing examples of determination over the term and then attaching the pictures to the tree as evidence. The tree can be reviewed on a weekly basis with sticky notes added when children demonstrate gumption. For example, 'Joe tried really hard with his maths today and stayed in to finish it' or 'Gemma helped a Year 1 child when she fell over in the playground today.'

The learning check could involve children writing about how they can 'grow more gumption' and sticking ideas and strategies on the gumption tree at the end of the lesson. The next lesson uses the tree to develop the children's thinking to the next stage.

Resources needed:

Film clips from *Forrest Gump*
Paper for drawing the gumption tree
Sticky notes for plenary
Writing paper
Coloured pencils

LESSON 10: GETTING MORE GUMPTION

Learning focus: To know how to develop your gumption and stick at things even when it gets tough.

> Gumption = mental toughness gained through common sense and hard work.

To get gumption we need to develop our *resilience*. This means having:

- Persistence
- Determination
- Sticking at it
- Ability to bounce back
- 'I can, I will.'

Here are some examples of gumption:

1. I got lost in the supermarket once and I couldn't find my mum. I was afraid and crying but I still managed to go to the customer services desk and ask them to call my mum.

2. I saw some boys being mean to a new reception child. They were teasing him and he looked sad. I went up and told them to leave him alone. I took him to meet some friendly children to cheer him up.

3. My computer game wouldn't work properly so I downloaded help from the internet and now it works.

Think of three examples of when you have shown gumption at home or at school:

1. ....

....

2. ....

....

3. ....

....

LESSON 10:
GETTING MORE GUMPTION PAGE 2

Learning focus: To know how to develop your gumption and stick at things even when it gets tough.

GROW YOUR GUMPTION

What do you say to yourself to help you 'grow your gumption'? Fill in the empty speech bubbles with helpful things to say to yourself:

Learning focus: To know how to develop your gumption and stick at things even when it gets tough.

Can you make up a song or a rap about gumption?

Now design a new tree called the gumption tree. Think about the roots, trunk, leaves and blossoms. Bobby has his own ideas for the tree.

> 'I want a gumption tree that has all my useful words and sayings growing on it like fruit. In the roots you can have the emotions that will help grow gumption. If you have it in your classroom it will always remind you how to be brave and resilient.'

Show all the things you have learned so far on your tree. Write the story of the tree to go with the picture: 'One day a tiny acorn was planted in a grassy field ... '

Put the gumption trees up in your classroom to remind you about how you can grow more gumption.

LESSON 10: GETTING MORE GUMPTION PAGE 4

Learning focus: To know how to develop your gumption and stick at things even when it gets tough.

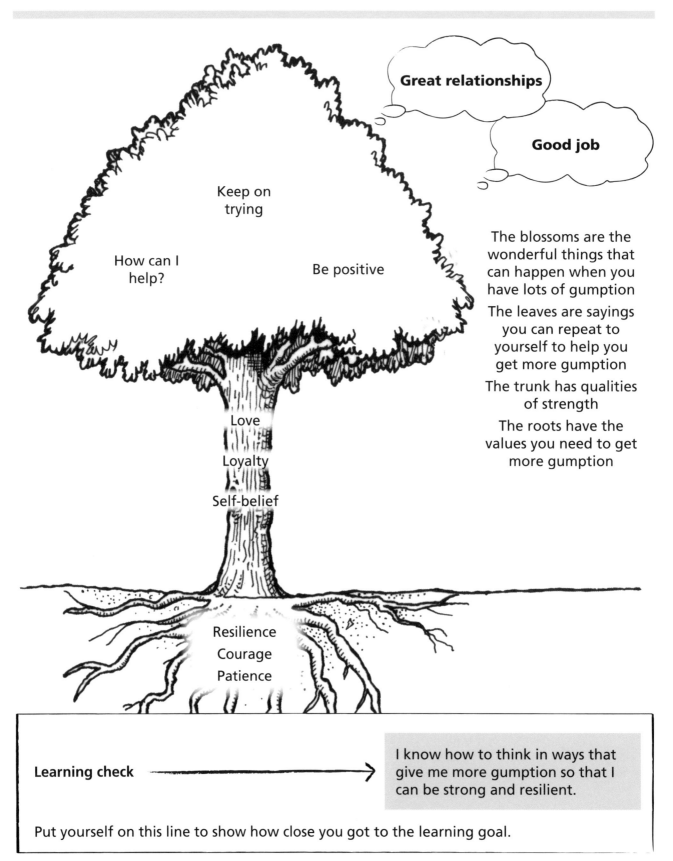

Great relationships

Good job

Keep on trying

How can I help?

Be positive

Love

Loyalty

Self-belief

Resilience

Courage

Patience

The blossoms are the wonderful things that can happen when you have lots of gumption

The leaves are sayings you can repeat to yourself to help you get more gumption

The trunk has qualities of strength

The roots have the values you need to get more gumption

Learning check ⟶ I know how to think in ways that give me more gumption so that I can be strong and resilient.

Put yourself on this line to show how close you got to the learning goal.

Teacher's Notes for Lesson 11: Believing in yourself

Learning focus: To know how to develop my strengths and build my confidence.

This lesson aims to develop gumption through increasing self-confidence and self-respect.

The first step to building confidence is to understand our own strengths and weaknesses. Children will be asked to judge their own confidence level then follow that up with a discussion about exactly what we mean by confidence. Can someone appear confident but underneath be shy? What is the body language of confidence?

The first task makes children think about their good points and what aspects they need to develop at school and at home. Then they need to think about how they can improve themselves by discussing their lists with their classmates – particularly by working with someone they don't know well. Children can ask questions and this encourages reflection. The idea is that pupils will have a chance to really consider what habits they have developed so far and what they could cultivate in the future.

The magic letter task develops empathy and self-confidence. By getting into the head of someone who loves them, the children can imagine what that person would say about them and wish for them. Bobby's example may help with this exercise.

The aim is that by the end of the lesson the children will be more aware of what their strengths are and how to build on them, and what their weaknesses are and how to use their strengths to address them.

Resources needed:

Lined paper for letter
Writing grids for the coaching exercise

LESSON 11: BELIEVING IN YOURSELF

Learning focus: To know how to develop my strengths and build my confidence.

Self-confidence will help you achieve real success *but* you have to know your weak spots too.

HOW CONFIDENT ARE YOU?

LOW	1	2	3	4	5	6	7	8	9	10	HIGH

Put a mark on this line to show where you are. Discuss with your partner why you have put yourself there.

 Discuss these questions:

- What is confidence?
- What do confident people look like?
- Can you be quiet and confident?
- What do confident people sound like?
- How do confident people think?
- What happens when you are over-confident?
- Trying walking into the room in a confident way – how does it feel?
- What is the opposite of confidence?

Liking and respecting yourself is the first step to being confident. Always start by being honest about *you*.

Get to know your best friend ... *you*.

LESSON 11: BELIEVING IN YOURSELF PAGE 2

Learning focus: To know how to develop my strengths and build my confidence.

 FIVE GOOD THINGS ABOUT ME

Start off by filling in five good things about yourself in the grid below. Then share your points with a friend and ask them if they agree with you. Get your friend to write in another good thing about you.

Five good things about me:
1.
2.
3.
4.
5.
My friend says:

LESSON 11:
BELIEVING IN YOURSELF PAGE 3

Learning focus: To know how to develop my strengths and build my confidence.

Now think about what you need to work on and fill in the grid below. Ask your friend again to add something else.

Three things I need to do to improve:
1.
2.
3.
My friend says I also need to improve on:

Now swap sheets with someone who doesn't know you very well. Talk about the answers they have written and think carefully about how they can improve.

Start by talking about the good things on the list. Ask about them and find out why these are on the list. Then ask about the improvement list. Try to get ideas from your classmate about how *they* think they could make these changes.

Share with the class the best advice you have been given by your partner.

LESSON 11: BELIEVING IN YOURSELF PAGE 4

Learning focus: To know how to develop my strengths and build my confidence.

 ## A MAGIC LETTER

Think of someone who cares for and loves you. Imagine that person is sitting at your desk now and is in control of your pen. Write a letter from that person to you, thanking you for being so great and celebrating your brilliance. Also include some reminders about things you need to watch out for (e.g. remember to tidy your bedroom more often). Include their hopes and dreams for your future. Keep this letter somewhere safe and read it whenever you want to feel confident.

....

....

....

....

....

....

....

....

....

....

....

....

....

....

....

....

LESSON 11: BELIEVING IN YOURSELF PAGE 5

Learning focus: To know how to develop my strengths and build my confidence.

Here is the letter Bobby received from his mum:

Dear Bobby,

I want to thank you for being such an amazing flying brain. When you were born I didn't realise you would grow up so brave and strong in character. I like the way you always believe you can have a go at everything, even though it is so hard for you with spindly arms and legs. I love the fact that you don't mind coming last in the race on sports day and you can just smile and laugh at yourself when you get things wrong. You are absolutely brilliant at thinking of funny ideas that help children to be better learners.

You can get really focused on what you are doing but sometimes you can be very forgetful and dizzy. I want to remind you to always make a list of what you have to do so that you don't forget something important.

I have a dream that you will be able to spread your work across the world to children of all different nationalities. I want you to be a super teacher and keep learning more about how to help others. Thank you for being you and keep up all the good work.

Love forever,

Mummy xx

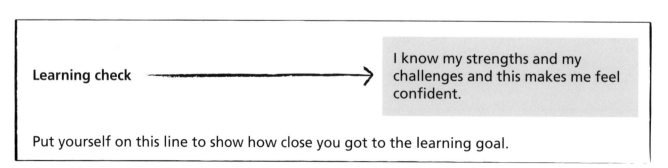

Learning check   ⟶   I know my strengths and my challenges and this makes me feel confident.

Put yourself on this line to show how close you got to the learning goal.

Teacher's Notes for Lesson 12: Be a stickability coach

Learning focus: I know how to help myself and others to stick at it when they are learning.

'Stickability' means persistence and resilience. Bobby gives an example of when he has found something difficult and has had to find a solution.

Thinking about babies learning to walk and talk demonstrates to the children that they have already shown amazing resilience in their lives. How did they do it? What is the habit of resilience – and how can we get more of it? Answering these questions is the aim of this lesson.

Sailing round the world is a good example of stickability and there have been several examples of youngsters who have recently taken on such challenges to discuss with the class.

The next task is to help the children practise coaching each other in a simple task. The key is that the coach assists the person to find answers for themselves. When children receive advice and guidance they reflect on what they need to improve, and keep working at it, so they build a resilience that can become a habit.

Sports coaches constantly give feedback, advice and set targets. The teacher can develop these types of coaching skills for developing gumption. This type of coaching is often given by parents at home on a regular basis but some children don't have this type of reinforcement so this lesson is even more important for them. The teacher may wish to demonstrate a coaching session to show the class before they start this part of the lesson. When sharing the best coaching practice it may be worth talking about sports coaches and how they help to develop skills through support and encouraging feedback.

For the coaching task the children have to draw a boat using the wrong hand and this immediately increases feelings of being outside their comfort zone and having to be resilient. The children are not meant to be judging if they are good at drawing but if they are good at helping others to do a difficult task, sticking with it and showing improvement. The DIRT acronym is catchy and helps remind us to do that Dedicated Improvement and Reflective Time.

The learning check is to ensure the children have developed strategies for how they will 'unstick' themselves the next time they get stuck.

Resources needed:

Writing paper
Video clips or pictures of sailing adventures
Plain paper for drawing

LESSON 12: BE A STICKABILITY COACH

Learning focus: I know how to help myself and others to stick at it when they are learning.

> *'Another word for persistence is "stickability". Stickability means you stick at things and don't give up easily. One thing about learning is that nothing sticks unless you practise it and work hard – even when you feel like giving up. I love stickability because even when I am stuck and feel like crying, it helps me grit my teeth and keep going till I "get it". The other day I was stuck with working out how to use my new computer. It just wouldn't work and I tried shouting and then sulking but in the end I got some help and I went back to the beginning and looked at my instructions and finally I got it! Whoopee – stickability is stupendous! When have you shown some stickability?'*

How do babies learn to walk? How do toddlers learn to talk? Write down a list of the stages for these.

What keeps them going? Why do *all* healthy babies learn to walk and *all* toddlers learn to talk? Why don't they give up as it's so hard? They have stickability! Stickability gives you gumption.

By training yourself in stickability you get more persistent – then you can become resilient and strong. Then you can have plenty of gumption. If you practise this enough it becomes a habit. Then you do it without having to think about it.

SURVIVING MY VOYAGE ROUND THE WORLD

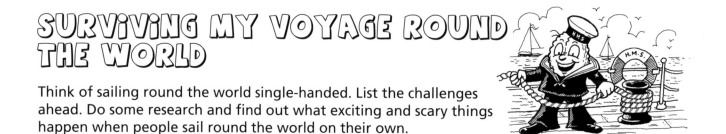

Think of sailing round the world single-handed. List the challenges ahead. Do some research and find out what exciting and scary things happen when people sail round the world on their own.

....

....

....

....

....

LESSON 12:
BE A STICKABILITY COACH PAGE 2

Learning focus: I know how to help myself and others to stick at it when they are learning.

For each of these challenges give some ideas of how you may advise someone to cope with their trip, such as loneliness, fear, danger or exhaustion.

....

....

....

....

....

....

....

....

....

....

....

'Sometimes you just have to grit your teeth and get on with it! It can be boring, tiring or scary but taking one step at a time and keeping going is the best way to succeed at anything. Whether you are sailing round the world or simply learning something new, you need resilience to succeed!'

LESSON 12: BE A STICKABILITY COACH PAGE 3

Learning focus: I know how to help myself and others to stick at it when they are learning.

BE A GREAT COACH

What is a coach? What qualities do you need to be a good one?

....

....

....

Now try them out …

Working in pairs, one of you draw a sailing boat with your wrong hand. The coach must give the artist advice and encouragement to improve the drawing and make them try at least two more times. Think about how you are improving during each attempt.

1.

2.

3.

Now swap drawings and see how coaching someone else has helped *you* improve. The best way of learning is by teaching someone else.

The Primary Learner's Toolkit © Jackie Beere and Crown House Publishing Ltd, 2010

Learning focus: I know how to help myself and others to stick at it when they are learning.

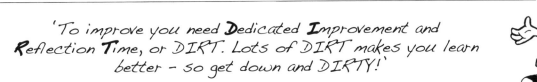

'To improve you need **D**edicated **I**mprovement and **R**eflection **T**ime, or DIRT. Lots of DIRT makes you learn better – so get down and DIRTY!'

BE A GREAT SELF-COACH

Now try writing with your eyes closed. Write your full name neatly. Try again and again until it is as good as when you can see the paper.

The most important question is: How can you be your own life coach to encourage persistence at home and at school? Find out why a coach makes such a difference to the way a team or individual performs.

Learning check ⟶	I know how to help myself and others to stick at it when they are learning.

Put yourself on this line to show how close you got to the learning goal.

Teacher's Notes for Lesson 13: Get more willpower

Learning focus: To know how to get more willpower when I need it.

Research shows it takes 10,000 hours of practice to become a great musician or racing driver (see *Outliers* by Malcolm Gladwell). The aim of this lesson is to develop the awareness that willpower is a habit that can help you achieve what you want. In our fast moving, hedonistic society we need to counteract the media messages that reinforce materialism and nurture short concentration spans by showing children how to train their brain to wait and use all the resources around them to break through barriers to learning.

In this lesson the children look at six steps to train their brains to wait and then think in pairs about applying them to something they would like to do.

The next part of the lesson looks at discussing strategies to develop willpower. These can be shared in pairs, then in the class and may be posted on the classroom wall. Games that develop willpower such as chess and patience or practical activities such as unicycling and juggling all require great applied willpower. Children can choose one to develop and consider for their willpower weekend.

The final exercise can be completed in teams. The activity weekend can consist of a venue, a list of events, a menu and some outcomes. The team can present their weekend and show how it would work to develop the willpower of participants. The class can vote on the most powerful programme before filling in their learning check.

Resources needed:

Writing paper for brain training steps
Large sugar paper to plan the willpower weekend

LESSON 13: GET MORE WILLPOWER

Learning focus: To know how to get more willpower when I need it.

How many hours of practice does it take to become really good at something?

Answer. 10,000. People who have great skill have practised for at least 10,000 hours to perfect it. That's about three hours a day, every day, for ten years!

Have you got the kind of willpower that could make you a genius? If you can train your brain to wait, then you will be a great learner, because learning takes practice and hard work.

'You can't always have what you want straight away but most successful people grow their motivation so they can work hard and keep trying until they reach their goal. I find the harder I work, the luckier I get!'

SIX STEPS TO TRAINING YOUR BRAIN TO WAIT

Step 1: Think about what you want to do and how good it will feel to be able to do it.

Step 2: Find out from experts and teachers how to do it.

Step 3: Make a plan to practise what you have learned every day.

Step 4: Practise every day and check your own progress. Practise some more.

Step 5: Show someone you trust what you are doing and get some good feedback to help you get better.

Step 6: Adjust your plan and repeat from Step 4 until you become brilliant.

LESSON 13: GET MORE WILLPOWER PAGE 2

Learning focus: To know how to get more willpower when I need it.

WILLPOWER TRAINING

How do you resist temptation? How do you put off doing what you want now for something better later? Discuss strategies for the following challenges with your neighbour and think of some good advice:

- You have a box of chocolates but you want them to last all week.

- You have to save up for some nice new trainers but it will take you two months' pocket money to do it.

- You find a big pile of Christmas presents in a cupboard ready for wrapping up and you want to look at them.

- You have to do your homework before you are allowed out to play.

Make a list of games and sports that can develop willpower. How can teamwork help your willpower?

....

....

....

....

....

....

....

....

....

....

LESSON 13:
GET MORE WILLPOWER PAGE 3

Learning focus: To know how to get more willpower when I need it.

 # WILLPOWER WEEKEND

Design an activity weekend that will help to train children in willpower. Explain each activity and how it will develop their willpower (e.g. learning a dance or building a shelter which both need lots of patience and determination).

Example programme for willpower weekend	Willpower activity
Arrive Friday at 6 p.m. for dinner, to include energy foods	Choose from the following to learn for one hour then demonstrate: Practise a karaoke song to perform Choreograph and perform a dance Create an exercise routine to teach your group later
Saturday	AM: 12 mile walk challenge through countryside to set destination PM: Circus skills workshop. Learn to juggle or unicycle Evening – reflection time. How did willpower help you?

No pain, no gain.
Take one for the TEAM!

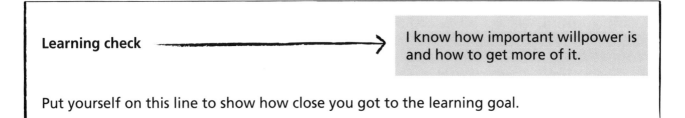

Learning check ⟶ I know how important willpower is and how to get more of it.

Put yourself on this line to show how close you got to the learning goal.

Teacher's Notes for Lesson 14: Bobby's brain blast

Learning focus: To find out how my brain works and how to make it work well for me.

The purpose of this lesson is to find out how powerful the brain is for learning. All the statements in Bobby's brain quiz are true and children may want to go home and find out more facts about the power of their brain.

On a large sheet of paper learners can write everything they know already about the brain. When this is complete it can be put aside. Later in a plenary they can add to the brain scan in a different colour to see how much progress they have made in learning about the brain.

The next part of the lesson is to consider all the things their own brain has to manage (e.g. breathing, digesting food, keeping balance, hearing sounds). There are some possible activities to try to engage the children in this learning about the brain (e.g. acting as brain cells that make connections as they learn a new skill).

Children can consider how they can stretch their brainpower. The goal is to learn new things and do things in different ways in the future. Finally the learners could do further research about the brain and prepare a presentation to share their findings.

After a return to the brain scan to add what they know now, the learning check at the end could review what the brain does and how amazing it is.

Resources needed:

Book box about the brain
Paper for drawing spider diagram/mindmap

LESSON 14: BOBBY'S BRAIN BLAST

Learning focus: To find out how my brain works and how to make it work well for me.

See what Bobby says about the brain and discuss which sentences you think are true:

LESSON 14:
BOBBY'S BRAIN BLAST PAGE 2

Learning focus: To find out how my brain works and how to make it work well for me.

 ## BRAIN SCAN
Write down everything you already know about your brain.

....

....

....

....

....

....

....

....

....

....

....

....

....

....

....

....

....

....

....

LESSON 14:
BOBBY'S BRAIN BLAST   PAGE 3

Learning focus: To find out how my brain works and how to make it work well for me.

Now, brainstorm all the things *your* brain has to do in a large spider diagram – or brain scan! (e.g. seeing where you are going, digesting your food, listening to the teacher).

LESSON 14:
BOBBY'S BRAIN BLAST PAGE 4

Learning focus: To find out how my brain works and how to make it work well for me.

 ## BRAIN STRETCH

The way to stretch your brain is to do something you don't normally do – something that will make your brain work in a different way. Here are some examples.

1. Watch a TV programme that makes you think (not your usual TV!).

2. Use a new word such as 'supercilious' (find out what it means first!).

3. Listen to some classical music and pick out the instruments.

4. Write with your wrong hand.

Write down three more ways you could stretch your brainpower this week:

1. ....

....

....

2. ....

....

....

3. ....

....

....

The Primary Learner's Toolkit © Jackie Beere and Crown House Publishing Ltd, 2010

Learning focus: To find out how my brain works and how to make it work well for me.

 Do some brain research! Find out more about your brain by looking in books and on the internet. Prepare a PowerPoint presentation to help teach your friends about the brain.

Go back to your brain scan and add some more things you *now* know about the brain in a different colour.

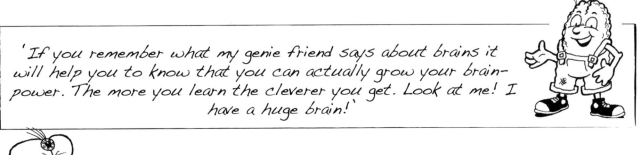

'If you remember what my genie friend says about brains it will help you to know that you can actually grow your brain-power. The more you learn the cleverer you get. Look at me! I have a huge brain!'

'Your brain is amazingly clever.' 'Your brain is as individual as your fingerprint.' 'You can grow your brain by learning.' 'Use it or lose it!'

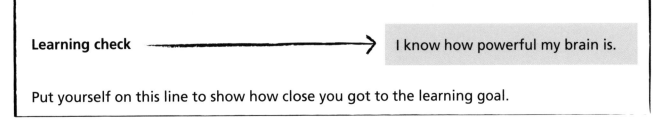

Learning check ⟶ I know how powerful my brain is.

Put yourself on this line to show how close you got to the learning goal.

Teacher's Notes for Lesson 15: The animals inside your brain

Learning focus: To know how to make your brain work well.

This lesson encourages the children make their brain work more effectively. It builds on work from Lesson 14 and presents a simple model of the three part brain (see MacLean 1990). The three parts of the brain are: the thinking brain (represented by the owl), the emotional brain (represented by the rabbit) and the reptilian brain – the primitive survival brain (represented by the crocodile). Lessons 15–17 aim to help the children understand how each part of the brain can help in the learning process.

It would be good to draw the owl, rabbit and crocodile or find suitable pictures and complete the activity that considers how each of the animals work together to contribute to our overall brain activity.

The lesson then focuses on the importance of controlling the reptilian brain. This is the part of the brain that downshifts into road rage or temper tantrums when challenged. Children can get into the habit of losing their temper and the purpose of this work is to help them take control and distract their brain from this spiral into a loss of control. Children can learn to develop anger management skills and avoid aggressive behaviours. It is useful to use puppets or toys to represent the owl, the rabbit and the crocodile as this makes it more memorable for children. For example, in this lesson the crocodile can talk to the learners about how angry he feels and why he doesn't want to learn because 'It's not fair!' or 'The teacher hates me!' or 'I can't do it!'

The learners can represent different responses in their plays to show how anyone can control their temper and create different outcomes.

The learning check should focus on strategies for managing the reptilian brain state.

Resources needed:

Paper and crayons
Poster paper
Rabbit, crocodile and owl puppets or toys

LESSON 15: THE ANIMALS INSIDE YOUR BRAIN

Learning focus: To know how to make your brain work well.

USING YOUR BRAIN

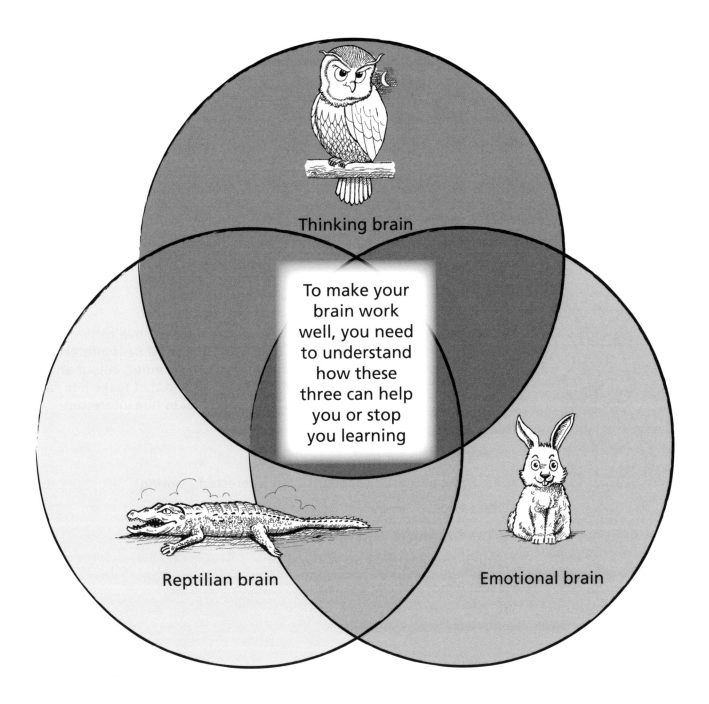

Thinking brain

To make your brain work well, you need to understand how these three can help you or stop you learning

Reptilian brain

Emotional brain

Learning focus: To know how to make your brain work well.

THINKING BRAIN

Your wise thinking brain is needed for reflecting and learning. The owl is sensible and hard working. Sometimes he is creative and dreamy when he's thinking and sometimes he prefers to be organised and do things in great detail.

Things he may say are:

- I can concentrate and think hard.
- I can ask good questions.
- I can check through my work carefully and spot mistakes.
- I can listen to the teacher.
- I can think of good ideas.

EMOTIONAL BRAIN

Your emotional brain is cuddly and loving and helps the owl to remember and learn things. But he only helps the owl if *he* is interested. He loves strange and funny things and adores praise, music, colour and sound – anything that gets his emotions working and that make him feel good. And anything that makes him feel good makes him interested.

Things he might say are:

- What is in this for me?
- No emotions getting sparked – not interested – boring!
- Have I done it well?
- I love colour and wacky pictures.
- Sing it to me to help me remember.
- I feel happy so I want to learn.

REPTILIAN BRAIN

Your reptilian brain can stop you learning if he takes control. He can take over if you feel threatened or unhappy. He makes you feel too angry to work and can get you into trouble because he makes you say or do things you don't mean. It's good to know how to calm him down so that you can get on with your work.

Learning focus: To know how to make your brain work well.

Things he might say:

- Why do I have to do this – it's too hard!
- I am too angry to work!
- I feel like storming out!
- You don't like me!
- I hate …!

What to do if you feel reptilian:

1. Write down three ways to calm yourself down and make a positive outcome more likely.

   ....

   ....

   ....

2. Write a set of slogans to say to yourself to your control anger.

   ....

   ....

   ....

3. Think of your brain as a computer with several different files that you can open or close. Imagine you have a file for different feelings such as 'happiness', 'curiosity' or 'determination'. Your reptilian brain state is the 'angry' file. Sometimes you get angry but you can learn to close down the file and deal with it later. This helps you have more control of your temper.

ROLEPLAY ACTIVITY

Make up two short plays. In the first one some friends fall out and one of them loses their temper. In the second one some friends fall out in the same way but they control their temper and it ends happily.

'When I feel angry it's easy to say nasty things and then I get more and more angry until I go red and sweaty and get into trouble. Now when I feel it coming on, I just think "close down the angry file" and open up the listening file. It's great because now I can keep calm and explain how I feel which makes people respect my views. I always try to remember to be a STAR: Stop – Think – Act – Review. It keeps me out of trouble!'

Learning focus: To know how to make your brain work well.

 Make a poster for your bedroom wall that will remind you about the reptilian brain and how it can take over – if you let it.

Learning check ────────────────→ I know how my brain works and how to control my reptilian brain.

Put yourself on this line to show how close you got to the learning goal.

The Primary Learner's Toolkit © Jackie Beere and Crown House Publishing Ltd, 2010

Teacher's Notes for Lesson 16: The rabbit rules

Learning focus: How to turn on your emotional brain.

This lesson aims to help children understand how to engage their emotional brain. By looking critically at magazine adverts they will be able to see how advertisers target their emotional brains to attract interest and then ensure people remember the products. Advertising uses colour, rhyme, music and emotions to do this.

The rest of the lesson is an exercise in using our powerful visual imaginations to make things easy to remember. This can be adapted for many things the children need to recall. Teachers could also include songs about the alphabet or times tables and show how they are more memorable when set to music.

The learning check should assess whether children now know how their emotional brain can help them to remember important things for their learning.

Resources needed:

Rabbit puppet or picture
Coloured pens
Examples of radio, TV and magazine advertisements

LESSON 16: THE RABBIT RULES

Learning focus: How to turn on your emotional brain.

THE EMOTIONAL BRAIN

The rabbit loves praise, music, rhyme, colour, funny and surprising things, and needs to see the point of learning.

Look at some advertisements in a magazine or think of some television or radio advertisements you can remember.

> How do advertisers make them memorable?
>
> Which part of your brain are they targeting?
>
> How do they do it? List the ways.

What is your earliest memory?

Try to remember what you have learned this term so far. You may find that you remember things with an emotional connection such as an argument or accident.

'Learn how to help your brain get interested and remember things so that you don't forget. Learning your times tables with a song makes them easy to remember. Try it!'

 # FOOD FOR THOUGHT

See if you can remember this healthy shopping list:

Carrots	4 yoghurts	Oranges
Newspaper	Milk	Tomatoes
Fruit juice	Lettuce	Potatoes
Washing powder	Tea bags	

LESSON 16: THE RABBIT RULES PAGE 2

Learning focus: How to turn on your emotional brain.

Now try remembering them all by making the list into a story – by turning on your emotional brain imagination and letting the rabbit rule!

Carrots	Imagine a giant orange carrot growing in the garden. Nibbling it are hundreds of white rabbits
Newspaper	A newspaper folded into the shape of an aeroplane flies in from above and knocks the carrot over
Fruit juice	As the carrot topples over litres of fruit juice start pouring out of the top cascading over all the white rabbits and turning them orange
Washing powder	Suddenly it's snowing masses of tiny particles of washing powder turning the rabbits back to white
4 yoghurts	A car screeches to a halt and out get four yoghurt pots with grinning faces. They march towards the rabbits in a line
Milk	....
Lettuce	....

LESSON 16:
THE RABBIT RULES PAGE 3

Learning focus: How to turn on your emotional brain.

Tea bags	....
Oranges	....
Tomatoes	....
Potatoes	....

You finish the story for the other items. Then try to remember the whole shopping list without looking by remembering the weird story.

LESSON 16:
THE RABBIT RULES PAGE 4

Learning focus: How to turn on your emotional brain.

LEARNING IS EMOTIONAL

You can remember things if you have made them funny or silly or if you made up a song about them. Even the most boring things can be made easy to remember.

Spelling 'necessary' is hard to remember – but **N**ever **E**at **C**akes, **E**at **S**alad **S**andwiches **A**nd **R**emain **Y**oung is easier to remember!

Bobby's top tips for how you can use your emotional brain to help you learn are:

1. Make it exciting, colourful and funny.

2. Use music or rhyme and rhythm to help you remember things.

3. Give yourself a reason for learning. If *you* care, it will count.

4. Set yourself goals for learning and reward your efforts.

5. Use your imagination to help you be a good learner.

TIP: Learning names is easy if you use alliteration, for example, Gentle George, Saucy Sarah, Perfect Paul or Mad Matthew.

Learning check —————————————→ I know how to use my emotional brain to help me remember.

Put yourself on this line to show how close you got to the learning goal.

Teacher's Notes for Lesson 17: The wise old owl knows how to think

Learning focus: Know how to make the most of your thinking brain.

This lesson aims to help the children reflect on how their 'thinking brain' can have different preferences or ways of working. The tendency is for either more academic or more creative types of processing. This is sometimes referred to metaphorically as the left and right side of the brain: the 'left-brained' preference being academic, logical and systematic, and the 'right-brained' preference being creative, intuitive and chaotic. This lesson considers the learner's natural preference and how to make the thinking brain work more effectively by ensuring their academic and creative brains work together for maximum learning.

It is often said that people tend to be either more creative or more logically minded. This lesson helps children to recognise their natural inclination and watch out for the pitfalls of being either too chaotic or too meticulous in their thinking. It is worth considering which category you fall into as a teacher. Are you creative, intuitive and dreamy, or logical, organised and scholarly? Or are you a bit of the best of both? Often the creative, chaotic thinkers can struggle at school with untidy work or disorganised planning, so it can help to know what the top tips are for challenging your brain to work with both preferences.

The children also have natural preferences in their thinking. There is no right or wrong but understanding your preferences can help learning. This lesson aims to help children understand their preferences and watch out for the challenges and opportunities that these present. Great learning needs creative *and* logical thinking.

As the children work through the lesson activities the final conclusion is about 'growing the brain' every day by challenging its established habits – going to school by a different route or watching an unusual television programme or sitting in an unfamiliar place in the staffroom – it's all good advice for staff as well as children!

The lesson ends with some 'thunks' (see Gilbert 2007).

The learning check is a chance to reflect on what the 'thinking' brain does best – get the children to think of some great questions to ask owl about learning as part of the plenary, such as 'How can I think better?'

Resources needed:

Owl puppet or picture
Paper

LESSON 17:
THE WISE OLD OWL KNOWS HOW TO THINK

Learning focus: Know how to make the most of your thinking brain.

'When I need to think hard I just consult the wise old owl in my brain and he helps me with difficult thinking.'

THE THINKING BRAIN

Your owl can be creative with lots of ideas but a bit disorganised.

Or your owl can be the logical well-organised type of thinker.

To be a *great* thinker you need a bit of both types of owl helping you be the best learner. You can find out which way your owl prefers to think by answering these questions yes or no:

1. I work step by step. ....
2. I can be impatient. ....
3. I like working on my own. ....
4. I like to make lists. ....
5. I can concentrate well. ....
6. I like reading. ....
7. I enjoy working with numbers. ....

More yes than no? You are more of a logical thinker. Owl has these top tips:

- Try new ways of working from time to time.
- Don't get bogged down in detail.
- Enjoy different things sometimes.
- Work with lots of other people.
- Have lots of ideas not just one.

LESSON 17:
THE WISE OLD OWL KNOWS HOW TO THINK PAGE 2

Learning focus: Know how to make the most of your thinking brain.

Now answer these questions yes or no:

1. I like to doodle a lot. ....

2. I love trying new ideas. ....

3. I like unfamiliar experiences. ....

4. I just try out ideas as I go along. ....

5. I prefer to flick through a magazine starting at the back. ....

6. I make decisions based on gut feelings. ....

7. I find it hard to concentrate quite often. ....

More yes than no? You are more of a creative thinker. Owl has these top tips:

- Don't forget details – do one step at a time.

- Make yourself do some planning and prioritising in advance.

- Avoid putting things off until the last minute.

- Listen carefully when given instructions.

- Don't rush in without thinking.

- Read instructions carefully.

- Check your work when you have finished.

'Don't get stuck in a rut! Boost your brain by trying something new every day: eat a food you don't normally eat, watch a different TV programme or speak to a person you don't usually talk to.'

Learning focus: Know how to make the most of your thinking brain.

The owl has lots of thinking tips that can help you learn:

Tips for being creative	Tips for making decisions
Think of **lots** of ideas	Weigh up the positive and negative
....	....
....	....
....	....
Tips for planning	**Tips for analysing**
Make a list	Ask good questions
....	....
....	....
....	....

Can you fill up each box with three more ideas?

Questions are great to make the owl practice thinking. Look at these questions

- Where does the sky start?
- Is a broken down car parked?
- What does happiness taste like?

Think of some more to challenge the owl.

....

....

....

Learning check ⟶ I know how to use my thinking brain for learning.

Put yourself on this line to show how close you got to the learning goal.

Teacher's Notes for Lesson 18: Charm offensive

Learning focus: To know how to be charming to everyone I meet.

The purpose of this lesson is to teach the good old-fashioned communication skills of charm and good manners – in a fun way. The lesson links charm with the origins of the word and this works well with the MAGIC theme.

The next activity aims to develop communication skills through an active approach to listening.

The subsequent activities experiment with body language and the good practices of great manners. Practising this explicitly and exaggerating the gestures could elicit a discussion about how it feels to deliver and receive good manners.

Making a charm mask gives the children an opportunity to act out a different personality without self-consciousness. This should also be a fun activity that can be taken home to practise the charm offensive on parents!

For the learning check the plenary could be for the children to introduce themselves to each other in a 'charming' way.

Resources needed:

Card, egg boxes, glue, paint, etc. to make a charm mask

LESSON 18: CHARM OFFENSIVE

Learning focus: To know how to be charming to everyone I meet.

'After you. Charm will get you everywhere – and it's so easy!'

Find out what the word 'charm' means. One meaning is magic. This makes charm a MAGIC communication skill. If you have charm then you will be able to get on with everyone. If you have charm you can also get *rapport* – this is a French word. Find out what it means.

'Be charming whenever you can as it will make you popular with everyone!'

FIVE STEPS TO BECOMING A LITTLE CHARMER

1. Listen to others very carefully and make it clear you are listening by smiling and nodding.

   Try it. In pairs tell a story of a holiday you enjoyed for three minutes. The storyteller is going to mark the person listening out of 10 for charming listening.

2. Have great manners. Greet people in a positive way. Open the door for others. Give out books for the teacher. Say please and thank you. Apologise if you do something wrong. Be nice and you will feel good.

   Try it tonight at home and see what a difference it makes.

3. Compliment others – and mean it! If your friend, teacher or sister looks nice, say so – and mean it. It doesn't count if you make it up. Take compliments well yourself too.

   Try it – give your friend a compliment and sound like you mean it.

4. Be enthusiastic and show it in your voice and body language. Ask questions and show an interest in other people.

   Try it – ask someone what they did at the weekend.

5. Smile and be friendly. It will make someone's day! When you smile you change your brain chemistry and attract people to you. Get in the habit of smiling!

LESSON 18: CHARM OFFENSIVE PAGE 2

Learning focus: To know how to be charming to everyone I meet.

MAGIC CHARM MASK

Make a MAGIC charm mask with a lovely smile, big eyes and a happy expression. Use it to act out being charming in different situations such as shopping, being on a train or in a restaurant.

How can you be charming to these different people?

- Your friends
- Your sisters and brothers
- Your mum and dad

- Your teachers
- Your neighbours
- People you don't know yet

KEY WORDS AND PHRASES TO REMEMBER:

Charm

Rapport

Listen

Smile

Please

Thank you

Sorry

Pardon me

After you

Do you need some help?

What can I do for you?

Learning check ⟶ I am able to be a charming communicator when I need to be.

Put yourself on this line to show how close you got to the learning goal.

Teacher's Notes for Lesson 19: Take one for the team

Learning focus: To know how to work well with others and communicate well in a team.

The purpose of this lesson is to help the children understand how to get on with others and be a great team player by understanding what attracts others to you. The children then consider what makes teams work well. At this point examples of teams (e.g. rowing, football, rock bands) could be discussed and roles within teams shared.

The next task is to consider the different roles in a team and what qualities are needed to perform each role. This is important preparation for group work on the learning projects in Section II. It is important that children get to try out different roles so they become flexible team players (e.g. leader, motivator, team coach, timekeeper).

The next activity involves drawing around their hands and writing a promise on each finger that links into the qualities discussed about being a great team player. These hands can be displayed as a promise board on the classroom wall.

The last activity, working in pairs, develops the theme of body language to practise mirroring and matching in a conversation to enhance the empathy that this type of communication can create.

The extension work would be for the children to do something at home that would involve working with each other to develop a charity project and raise some money for a community organisation.

The learning check will confirm the children's understanding of what makes a great team player. This prepares them well for the collaborative work in Section II of this book, which will develop their learning skills and habits.

Resources needed:

Paper for drawing their hands
Paper or card to create a promise board to stick the hands on
Coloured pens/paints for the drawing

LESSON 19: TAKE ONE FOR THE TEAM

Learning focus: To know how to work well with others and communicate well in a team.

'I love working in a team and sharing success but sometimes it is hard to get on with others and I can feel shy or frustrated when working with people I don't know very well.'

Being a good team player is one of the main skills employers look for when recruiting. Sometimes that means putting your own needs or views second for the good of the team. It also means being able to bring out the best in others.

Think of two examples where you have put someone else's needs before your own.

1. ....

....

....

....

....

2. ....

....

....

....

LESSON 19: TAKE ONE FOR THE TEAM PAGE 2

Learning focus: To know how to work well with others and communicate well in a team.

Tick which of these characteristics would make you want to choose someone for your team for a school project:

You work hard	You listen to others	You don't mind doing the harder jobs	You are enthusiastic	You help others join in
You talk the most	You like to be a leader	You have the best trainers	You try to offer ideas	You make everyone laugh
You concentrate well	You are good at football	You can write neatly	You will try anything to help the group	You join in

Finish this sentence:

'My ideal team mate is ....'

In a team what are the important roles *you* could play? Write in the box what would be the important qualities and jobs for each of these roles.

Leader ....

Motivator ....

Quality control manager ....

Coach ....

Time manager ....

Learning focus: To know how to work well with others and communicate well in a team.

How do some people *stop* the team working well?

....

....

....

....

YOUR PROMISE TREE

Draw around your hand on a piece of paper.

On each finger write a promise that will help you work well in a team. In the centre of the hand write a poem or slogan to motivate the team. Create a promise tree using the hands of the whole class.

Learning check ⟶ I know how to be a good team player that others want to work with.

Put yourself on this line to show how close you got to the learning goal.

The Primary Learner's Toolkit © Jackie Beere and Crown House Publishing Ltd, 2010

Teacher's Notes for Lesson 20: Leadership MAGIC

Learning focus: Know how to be a good leader of a team.

The purpose of this lesson is to prepare children for the project work in Section II by encouraging them to think about the skills of leadership. Being a leader is about listening and inspiring others as well as having a strong personality. This lesson builds on Lesson 19 on team member skills.

Looking at some of our leaders across the world is a good starter. The children will see how much criticism leaders can experience and this emphasises the accountability aspect of leadership.

The activity where the children break down the skills in more detail should encourage a sense of what the key communication skills needed to be a good leader are (e.g. speaking clearly, checking things get done).

For the next activity, the teacher could give groups the challenge and the context for the leadership speeches to be developed. The speeches can be filmed for class analysis if there are willing volunteers.

The final challenge means taking all that the children have learned about team leadership and teamwork and putting it into a presentation for other children.

The extension work is a practical task with mirroring and matching to develop rapport with each other. This could be used if children need extra help with understanding how they communicate and develop empathy.

The learning check can be part of the assessment of the presentation given by the teams.

Resources needed:

Pictures of world leaders
Planning paper
Video cameras to film the speeches

LESSON 20: LEADERSHIP MAGIC

Learning focus: Know how to be a good leader of a team.

'Being a leader is a tough job but you only get good at it by being willing to have a go and practising! All teams can benefit from having a good leader but how can you get to be one?'

Look at some pictures of leaders. Name some leaders that you know (e.g. the Queen, Prime Minister, President of the United States, captain of the England football team). What have they got in common?

....

....

....

....

What does a leader have to do?

....

....

....

How does a leader have to look?

....

....

....

Why do we need leaders?

....

....

....

Learning focus: Know how to be a good leader of a team.

Write a list of qualities of good leaders.

....

....

....

....

....

....

....

....

....

....

Make a list of the good and bad things about being the leader.

....

....

....

....

....

....

....

....

....

....

LESSON 20:
LEADERSHIP MAGIC PAGE 3

Learning focus: Know how to be a good leader of a team.

 What are leadership skills and how do you get them? Fill in the boxes below with ideas of how you get the qualities in the headings on the left. Then add some more qualities of your own.

Taking responsibility	....	....
Inspiring the team	....	....
Organising jobs	....	....
	....	....
	....	....

LESSON 20:
LEADERSHIP MAGIC PAGE 4

Learning focus: Know how to be a good leader of a team.

BODY TALK

Body talk can help you be a good leader. Body talk is the way you stand, the way you look, what you wear and your facial expressions.

Make a list of the body language that helps good leadership of a team.

....

....

....

....

....

....

....

....

Practise mirroring body language to get better communication skills with a partner you don't know. Ask them three questions about themselves. Keep eye contact. Mirror their body position. Smile and nod. Keep your shoulders back and your head up. Listen carefully and feedback what they say to show you understand.

 GROUP CHALLENGE

In a group imagine you are a team that has to achieve one of the following challenges:

- Climb Mount Everest
- Win the next basketball or cricket match to get through to the finals
- Cook and serve a wonderful meal in a competition
- An idea of your own.

LESSON 20:
LEADERSHIP MAGIC PAGE 5

Learning focus: Know how to be a good leader of a team.

 Discuss your team activities and consider what the team may be thinking and feeling as they prepare for the challenge. Act out the *team talk* with each of you taking it in turns to be the leader. Film some of the leaders' talks with a video camera. Fill out this card for each leader's talk.

Praise comment about the leader's talk	Advice comment about the leader's talk
....	....
....	....
....	....
....	....

LESSON 20: LEADERSHIP MAGIC PAGE 6

Learning focus: Know how to be a good leader of a team.

Now plan a team presentation about leadership. You can use examples of leaders you know and what makes a great leader. You can show what your top tips are for developing leadership skills. Use drama, ICT or posters to help your talk. Decide who will lead this group activity. Present it to other year groups.

BOBBY'S TOP TIPS:

Work with as many different people every day as you can – don't just work with your friends.

Be 'proactive' in making new friends. In other words, talk to people and don't just wait for people to talk to you.

Keep your body language open, make eye contact and always smile.

Ask questions with interest and listen closely to the answers.

Learning check ⎯⎯⎯⎯⎯⎯⟶ I know how to develop leadership skills.

Put yourself on this line to show how close you got to the learning goal.

Teacher's Notes for Lesson 21: Learning detectives

Learning focus: To be able to ask good questions about our learning.

Being a good communicator is about asking good questions and listening carefully. This lesson tries to sum up the enquiry ethos that this toolkit has engendered in the classroom. The best learners are curious and this session aims to encourage an enquiry-based classroom.

It begins by examining curiosity and moves on to a survey about learning and how it works for different children. The survey can be as simple or complex as the age group or ability of the class dictates. The evidence can include graphs and link to ICT or could just be photographs taken with a digital camera. As homework, children could ask questions at home about learning and include their hobbies and leisure activities.

The poster would be an excellent display item and should focus on good questions. A literacy opportunity relating to questioning could present itself with older classes. This could include open and closed questions, knowledge and evaluation questions.

The learning check is to reflect on how well the children have developed an awareness of what questions need to be asked to be good at learning enquiry.

Resources needed:

Access to computers
Digital cameras
Coloured pencils/pens and paper for poster

LESSON 21: LEARNING DETECTIVES

Learning focus: To be able to ask good questions about our learning.

'When we keep wondering about learning and thinking about how it works it helps us be better learners – so I want you to become a learning detective and develop your curiosity. If you can become a learning detective it will make you a great learner for life!'

WHAT DO YOU NEED TO BE A LEARNING DETECTIVE?

Curiosity – find out the Latin meaning.

How can curiosity help learning?

'Curiosity killed the cat.'

How can curiosity kill the cat?

What makes you curious?

Asking questions and thinking about the answers will make you a great learning detective.

LESSON 21: LEARNING DETECTIVES PAGE 2

Learning focus: To be able to ask good questions about our learning.

In teams you are going to investigate how other children learn. Make up a questionnaire with ten questions you can ask other learners in your class or school.

Ask questions about their learning at school *and* at home such as:

- How do you learn best?
- What do you learn from your friends?
- How does your teacher help you to learn?
- What motivates you to want to learn?
- When do you learn at home?
- What stops you learning?

Make up some of your own questions too! If you can ask some adults about their learning it will make you an even better detective!

1. ....

2. ....

3. ....

4. ....

5. ....

6. ....

7. ....

8. ....

9. ....

10. ....

When you read all the results of your survey think about how you could present what you have found out – in graphs or showing pictures of people learning or using quotes of what some of the learners said. Share your results with the class.

LESSON 21:
LEARNING DETECTIVES PAGE 3

Learning focus: To be able to ask good questions about our learning.

 # WE ARE LEARNING DETECTIVES

As learning detectives we ask questions, we wonder why and we want to know. Create a poster full of *your* questions about learning. Make it colourful, bright and include pictures too!

Learning check ————————————➤ I can ask good questions about learning.

Put yourself on this line to show how close you got to the learning goal.

Teacher's Notes for Lesson 22: Get the MAGIC right

Learning focus: To review everything you have learned in your toolkit so that you can teach it to younger children.

The purpose of this lesson is for the children to review the learning that has taken place in these sessions and prepare materials to make a presentation or teach their own lesson about the MAGIC habits.

This is a useful opportunity to recall what MAGIC stands for and what it means. The class can also make up stories similar to those Bobby Brain uses to support the themes in this book (see Section III).

The learning check will be part of the assessment of the presentation which is prepared to deliver to younger learners. This can be assessed by peer evaluation and teacher assessment. A box with success criteria is included for this purpose.

At the end of this lesson the children will be ready to go on to Bobby's Magic Towers in Section III – a collaborative activity to develop their learning skills further.

Resources needed:

Large paper for visual aids
ICT for research or PowerPoint presentation

LESSON 22: GET THE MAGIC RIGHT

Learning focus: To review everything you have learned in your toolkit so that you can teach it to younger children.

'**M**y motivation – I want to learn!'

'**A**ttitude – have a positive attitude.'

'**G**umption – stick at it and grow your confidence.'

'**I**-learn – use your brain for great learning.'

'**C**harming communication – impress everyone.'

> Use MAGIC to be a great learner.

Get into small groups and on a large sheet of paper create a colourful design that shows all you have found out about the MAGIC habits for learning. Imagine using it to teach younger children all about the habits. When you have completed it, present it to the class and show how you would use it to instruct other children. As you listen to each group's presentation, write a comment in each of these boxes:

	Success criteria	My praise and advice comment
Content	All the MAGIC habits were described clearly Good visual aids made it easier to understand It lasted more than three minutes	....
Communication skills	Clear voices All the team took part Positive body language	....

Learning check ⟶ I know how to be a great learner and can teach others about the MAGIC habits.

Put yourself on this line to show how close you got to the learning goal.

BRAIN BOOSTERS

Your brain and body are connected.

Try some of these physical exercises that challenge your brain.

- Stand up, stretch, reach up and breathe deeply to give your brain oxygen.
- Rub your tummy with one hand, pat your head with the other.
- Do the twist – arms one way, legs the other way.
- Draw a large figure of eight in the air with one finger.
- With one hand trace a circle moving outwards from your body. Use the other hand to trace a circle inwards towards your body. Keep them both going at the same time.
- Put your fingertips together very lightly and imagine connections being made between the right and left sides of your brain.
- Fold your arms. Now do it the other way – repeat until it feels comfortable each way.
- Write your full name with your wrong hand in large letters.
- Write your name with both hands creating a mirror image.
- Try writing your name backwards with your wrong hand.
- Create an impressive signature then copy it with your wrong hand.
- Throw your pen from one hand to the other and back again.

Now think of some of your own brain boosters.

HAVE A BRAIN/BODY WORKOUT

Imagine you are at the gym and a huge set of weights is in front of you. *In your mind* see yourself in full gym kit looking strong and happy, bending your knees and picking up the weights. Lift the weights slowly, keeping your back straight. Then raise the weights to your shoulders. Feel the weight, feel your strength. When you are steady lift them above your head and straighten your arms. Feel the weights for a few seconds then place them carefully back to your shoulders. Do this ten times then place them carefully back on the floor. This mental exercise can make you stronger in the real world.

Section II
Cross-Curricular Projects

- Implementing a creative curriculum through cross-curricular projects
- Developing social and emotional intelligence
- Creating independent, confident and lifelong learners

Introduction to the projects

This section contains six cross-curricular projects, specifically designed to complement the lessons in this book. They consist of a theme and scheme of work showing links to the primary curriculum subjects. The principle of the pedagogy in these projects is to encourage collaboration, choice and challenge. Each project has a strong focus on teamwork and gives students some element of choice in their work.

Learners should reflect on their progress in the essential life skills at suitable points during and at the end of the activity. These projects can be used and adapted for all age groups but middle and upper age primary would be particularly suited to the challenges. These tasks aim to engage the learners in real contexts that would interest them whilst helping them to progress with their essential learning skills.

It is hoped that these projects will also involve trips, visits and guest speakers whenever possible to connect the learning to the real world.

Each project concludes with a production or presentation involving parents or other students. This is a chance for learners to demonstrate their learning and communicate with other age groups.

Project 1: Bobby's Magic Towers

This project encourages the children to use the skills developed in the Learning Habits Toolkit lessons in Section I to design a theme park that will develop gumption and resilience. It entails researching what makes theme parks popular and successful. This activity gives ample opportunity for discussions about managing feelings and thrill seeking. The challenge of creating a theme park will encourage learners to look back at their work in the previous lessons and use any ideas that help. The learning from the MAGIC lessons will be reinforced and then can be applied in all six projects. Learners can create classroom displays to help them remember the neuroscience of how learning works which they can then refer back to later in the year.

Project 2: Exodus

This project can help to deliver some of the humanities content from the national curriculum. It looks at the movement and settlement of people over time and into the future. Learners examine the impact of other exodus and examine why people move around the planet. The project also addresses the problems of sustainable life on earth and possible solutions. The main collaborative activity is for learners to examine their own communities and how and why they work. This task is very much designed for the teacher to choose an appropriate direction according to the context of the school. The community discussed can be anything from a village to a district, school or estate, depending on the locality. The alien characters in the project want to give whole human communities the chance to move to Planet Zeal. The teacher and pupils will need to discuss the nature of community and their own area's strengths and weaknesses. Making the decision about whether to go to Planet Zeal or stay on Planet Earth will be an engaging debate. In the demonstration section, learners can use state-of-the-art technology to publish their work (e.g. blogs, podcasts or YouTube videos).

Project 3: The Wedding Plan

This project covers many subject areas and personal well-being outcomes, as it is concerned with relationships and partnerships (and can also cover sex education). It deals with the complex issues of parenting and family relationships. There are opportunities to invite in guest speakers with expertise on healthy eating, parenting or sexual development.

Learners have an opportunity to study weddings in various faiths and to understand the rituals involved before planning their own event. The wedding can be for an imaginary or a celebrity couple, with all the relevant themes and budgets. The children's ideas form a wedding exhibition which makes up the presentation at the end of the project. The work they produce on parenting can be offered to any parent visitors during the presentation.

Project 4: Disaster

This project includes many of the learning objectives from science and technology as well as issues of well-being and sustainability. The learners can choose which type of disaster to focus on. Older children may concentrate on one man-made disaster and one natural disaster. Survival is the theme of the project and there are lots of opportunities for discussion about resilience and motivation to link back to the MAGIC lessons. The practical aspect of this activity involves children choosing an artefact to make that will aid survival following a disaster. This could be a fishing rod, a manual about lighting fires, a boat or a bed – anything that will help people survive following a disaster. It could be made into a prototype or simply designed on a computer or on paper. Teachers may choose to create survival kits as an alternative, if practical work is not feasible.

Project 5: International Restaurant

In this project learners will be investigating the world of catering and culture through creating a restaurant with an international theme. It is an opportunity to link in the foreign languages aspect of the national curriculum and address health and well-being issues by applying learning to a service industry. It offers an easy way to bring in local chefs or restaurant proprietors for demonstrations. It also introduces the notion of good customer service which links into effective communication skills.

Learners will have an opportunity to investigate local restaurants and the eating habits of their own community. Various opportunities for addressing healthy eating and health and safety aspects of the workplace will be presented by this project. There are many opportunities to deliver group outcomes and learn about the power of teamwork as they plan their own international restaurant together and demonstrate their ideas to an audience of parents at the end of the task.

Project 6: The Time Machine

This is a very ambitious project that aims to engage learners in linking science, history and creativity in a very powerful way. It begins with teaching children about the way light and sound travel and then connects the science facts with the science fiction of time travel.

Learners can work together to design imaginary time machines, which links to developing design skills and creativity. Once the time machine is designed then the prospect of travelling back in time to research heroes from the past and learn from them makes a powerful connection with social understanding. Groups can choose their own historical figure to research and present their work to each other. Distilling what we can learn from past events and personalities will tie in powerfully with the personal learning skills that underpin all six projects. Teachers can decide the exact format of the final presentation – it could, for example, take the form of an assembly for younger children.

Bobby's Magic Towers

Project title and introduction

BOBBY'S MAGIC TOWERS

In this project you have to create a theme park with a difference – one that will help children to use all the MAGIC learning from this book. The theme park will create the MAGIC habits of Motivation, Action, Gumption, I-learn and Communication.

Activity number	Activity overview	Learning objectives	Possible outcomes	Essentials for learning and life	Some examples of KS2 National Curriculum Programmes of Study covered
1 Estimated time 6 hours	Set up the activity Investigate what makes a great theme park and an interesting museum (e.g. hands-on interactive displays, 3-D cinemas, demonstrations). Share activities ideas and organise a trip to a local attraction. Share publicity materials and good and bad experiences	■ To investigate why theme parks are popular and what elements make them successful ■ To research theme parks and museums ■ To consider ideas for new and original activities to make the theme park even better ■ To link this with the MAGIC habits so that the theme park activity helps to develop emotional intelligence	■ Creative writing about particular rides, displays, interactive displays, etc. ■ List of dangers and opportunities of theme parks ■ Health and safety rules ■ Extension work: research experiences of theme parks outside of school	Literacy/ICT Creative thinking	En1 En2 En3 En5 ICT 1, 2 PSHE/Cit 3e

Activity number	Activity overview	Learning objectives	Possible outcomes	Essentials for learning and life	Some examples of KS2 National Curriculum Programmes of Study covered
2 Estimated time 8 hours	In teams, plan your own Magic Towers theme park Include activities that will improve thinking skills, learning skills, emotional intelligence, charm and motivation (see activity sheet) Research where it should be situated in the country	◼ To develop ideas for rides and experiences that will promote personal and social skills ◼ To show awareness of a suitable location for the park	◼ List the ideas for the Magic Towers theme park ◼ Members of the group can complete chosen activities from sheet ◼ Draw a bird's eye map of the Magic Towers site	Thinking, learning and social skills Literacy Personal and emotional skills Teamwork	En1 En2 En3 Ge 1d Ge 3c, g DT 1
3 Estimated time 3 hours	Produce a publicity plan for your theme park Present it to the class Critically assess each others' publicity plan and the ideas for the theme park using the evaluation sheet	◼ To demonstrate creative approaches to various multimedia products that demonstrate the Magic Towers experience ◼ To present ideas that encapsulate the ethos of the theme park ◼ To incorporate an understanding of the personal and learning skills which are being developed in the theme park	◼ Produce the following advertising materials for the theme park and show how they display the MAGIC habits of Motivation, Action, Gumption, I-learn and Communication: • Leaflets for each activity • Posters/billboards • Magazine advert • Radio advert • TV storyboard • Video presentation • Web page • PowerPoint show	Literacy Fluency ICT Social skills Teambuilding skills Constructive support and feedback	En1 En2 En3 ICT 1 ICT 2 a ICT 3 a, b ICT 4

Activity number	Activity overview	Learning objectives	Possible outcomes	Essentials for learning and life	Some examples of KS2 National Curriculum Programmes of Study covered
4 Estimated time 3 hours	Come to Magic Towers! Create your own mini-version of the theme park at your school. Each group chooses one activity to run as a stall Invite parents in to try out the activities	■ To demonstrate adaptability and awareness of the development of MAGIC skills	■ Each stall will display artefacts to show some of the experiences enjoyed in the theme park	Communication skills Teamwork ICT	En1 Ar DT 2

BOBBY'S MAGIC TOWERS THEME PARK – YOUR TEAM CAN CHOOSE WHICH TASKS TO DO:

Choose to complete six of these and create the ride .

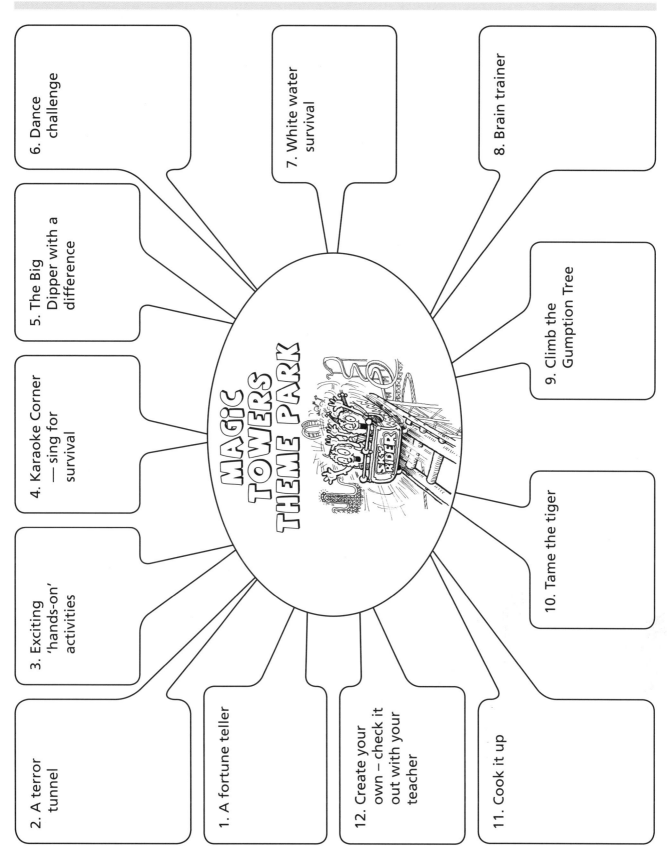

6. Dance challenge

7. White water survival

8. Brain trainer

5. The Big Dipper with a difference

4. Karaoke Corner — sing for survival

MAGIC TOWERS THEME PARK

9. Climb the Gumption Tree

3. Exciting 'hands-on' activities

10. Tame the tiger

2. A terror tunnel

1. A fortune teller

12. Create your own – check it out with your teacher

11. Cook it up

Example of Bobby's Magic Towers theme park activity sheet: Fortune Teller

Name of the activity	What you have to do (include pictures)	How much it costs
Meet Aunt Mabel the MAGIC white witch and create your own future	You go into a relaxation room and have a nice massage with soothing music in the background As you wait for Mabel, you relax in a room with changing lights and smells to sensitise you Mabel then comes in dressed in a psychedelic robe with her huge crystal ball. She asks you what you want to achieve and shows you in her crystal ball how it all comes true	£2
Who will like it Teenagers and mums	**How it helps develop MAGIC habits** It gets you in a relaxed, optimistic mood and then makes you think about your hopes and dreams. Planning these with Mabel will give you the confidence and motivation to make it all come true	
What people say about it	'I loved this activity as it made me feel so good about myself. Mabel was a lovely lady who is truly magical' 'What I liked best was the way it gave me time in my busy life to think about my dreams – now I know they will come true' 'I don't know how she did it but Mabel predicted that I was going to start enjoying school even though I had found it really hard since we moved house. And she was right. Since I went to see Mabel things have really changed for the better'	

Exodus

Project title and introduction	EXODUS
	NEWS FLASH! Planet Earth has been invaded by friendly aliens from Planet Zeal. The aliens have been watching us for many thousands of years and can see that within a hundred years we will not be able to live on our planet due to lack of resources, food and global warming. The aliens want to help, so they are offering humans sanctuary on their planet. But they *only* want to take whole communities to Planet Zeal. Half of the communities on Planet Earth must go to Planet Zeal if we are all to survive. All communities have to present a full account of their strengths and weaknesses, what they value and what they would like to change. This is your chance to go or stay. Which will it be?

Activity number	Activity overview	Learning objectives	Possible outcomes	Essentials for learning and life	Some examples of KS2 National Curriculum Programmes of Study covered
1 Estimated time 6 hours	Discuss what is meant by a community Research the impact of past exodus on existing communities Present your findings to whole group	■ To define 'community' ■ To examine various sources of information about previous exodus ■ To analyse the impact of previous exodus on communities ■ To demonstrate some understanding of people's actions on each other	■ Definitions of what a community is and what makes it work ■ Investigation of Vikings or Romans to discover the impact of their exodus in Britain ■ What is the impact of an exodus on the invaded people? ■ Migration – where have you lived and been? Global connections. How this relates to the above ■ PowerPoint presentations produced to share	Thinking and social skills	Hi 4a, b Hi 2c Hi 5c Hi 8a Hi 9 ICT 1 En1 PSHE/Cit 2d, g, h, i PSHE/Cit 4b

Activity number	Activity overview	Learning objectives	Possible outcomes	Essentials for learning and life	Some examples of KS2 National Curriculum Programmes of Study covered
2 Estimated time 5 hours	Discuss whether what the aliens say will happen to Planet Earth is true Discuss the range of problems facing humanity and possible solutions to them	■ To investigate problems facing humanity and possible solutions to them (e.g. whether Planet Earth is over-populated) ■ To consider reasons for leaving or staying ■ To consider how a community would decide to leave for a life on another planet	■ Drawing or computer graphics of the aliens ■ Speech from the alien leader ■ Description and outline of Planet Zeal ■ Record reasons why Planet Earth is over-populated etc. ■ Discuss initial reasons to go and stay ■ Speech from a community leader ■ Extension work: create a profile of Planet Zeal	Literacy ICT	Ge 5a, b Sc2, 5a PSHE/Cit 1a PSHE/Cit 2a, j En1 En2 En3

Activity number	Activity overview	Learning objectives	Possible outcomes	Essentials for learning and life	Some examples of KS2 National Curriculum Programmes of Study covered
3 Estimated time 6 hours	Either invent a community or research your own local community and how it is governed What do you want to keep in your community? Say why your community should stay or go with the aliens Fill in the community profile sheet for your chosen community Choose six tasks from the activity sheet Debate about the pros and cons of living on Planet Earth	■ To investigate what a local community is and how it works best by finding out about local democracy, e.g. parish councils	■ Deciding what community they will work with (e.g. school, village, suburb, town). Complete the activity sheet by choosing the various outcomes that illustrate your community ■ Complete community profile sheet ■ Listing pros and cons of staying on Planet Earth in your community or moving to Planet Zeal	Literacy Social skills Teambuilding skills	PSHE/Cit 1a PSHE/Cit 2b, g, h PSHE/Cit4, f
4 Estimated time 3 hours	Shall we go or shall we stay? As a group prepare a presentation that shows the aliens just what your community has to offer and whether you want to stay or go Parents can be invited in for the talk	■ To demonstrate awareness of the sustainability of communities and the importance of social cohesion and cooperation	■ A drama, dance or spoken presentation that shows whether your community should stay or go ■ A podcast, blog or YouTube video to demonstrate your community profile	Communication skills Teamwork ICT	Ar 2, c Ar 3a, b En1 En3 PSHE/Cit 2g ICT 2a ICT 4a, b, c

EXODUS – YOUR TEAM CAN CHOOSE WHICH TASKS TO DO:

Choose to complete six of these tasks in your team.

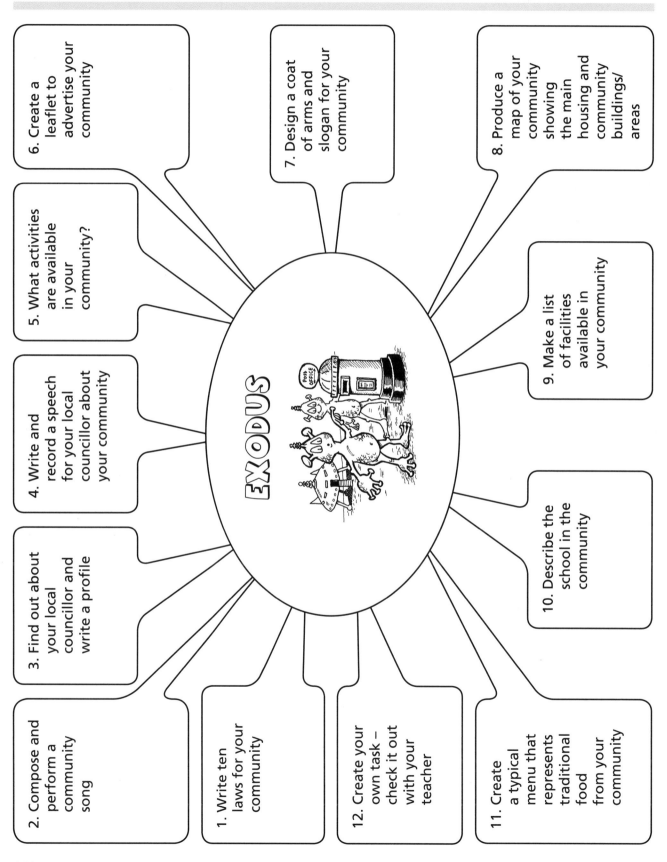

6. Create a leaflet to advertise your community

7. Design a coat of arms and slogan for your community

8. Produce a map of your community showing the main housing and community buildings/areas

5. What activities are available in your community?

4. Write and record a speech for your local councillor about your community

9. Make a list of facilities available in your community

3. Find out about your local councillor and write a profile

10. Describe the school in the community

2. Compose and perform a community song

1. Write ten laws for your community

12. Create your own task – check it out with your teacher

11. Create a typical menu that represents traditional food from your community

Example of community profile sheet

Name of our community and who belongs to it	Reasons for our community to go to Planet Zeal	Reasons for our community to stay on Planet Earth
Who is in our team	What we have to offer Planet Zeal	What we have to offer Planet Earth

How will we demonstrate our decision for the final production of our Exodus project

The Wedding Plan

Project title and introduction	THE WEDDING PLAN
	In this project learners will be planning an amazing wedding day. This links into the health and well-being area of learning as it covers relationships, parenting and community rituals. The opportunity to look at weddings in other cultures can give a global perspective. The production at the end can involve parents, with the wedding exhibition showing off cultural diversity in the context of the school community.

Activity number	Activity overview	Learning objectives	Possible outcomes	Essentials for learning and life	Some examples of KS2 National Curriculum Programmes of Study covered
1 Estimated time 6 hours	Research different types of weddings including religious ceremonies, civil services, etc. Examine the reasons why people get married and the history of the ritual	▪ To investigate the common features of marriage ceremonies ▪ To consider changes over time and cultural factors related to wedding ceremonies ▪ To link this with psychological aspects of commitment and partnership ▪ To consider the role of sex and reproduction inside and outside of marriage	▪ Watch some ceremonies, share ideas and gather evidence of a variety of weddings across the class ▪ Make a list of the common rituals and their purpose ▪ Make a list of the advantages and disadvantages of getting married ▪ Produce some graphs that show how marriage data has changed over the last hundred years (e.g. age at marriage) ▪ Nurse to talk to students about sex education ▪ Extension work: research at home about what weddings have been enjoyed and why	Literacy/ICT SEAL	PSHE/Cit 2a, e, i PSHE/Cit 4b, c, f ICT 1a, b ICT 3a, b Sc2, 1a Sc2, 2f Hi 2a, b En1 En2 En3

Activity number	Activity overview	Learning objectives	Possible outcomes	Essentials for learning and life	Some examples of KS2 National Curriculum Programmes of Study covered
2 Estimated time 8 hours	In teams plan a wedding and all the elements of it. Choose either a civil or a religious ceremony, venue, outfits, form of ceremony, menu, entertainments, honeymoon, etc. using the task sheet below	■ To use knowledge from the previous task to design a successful wedding day for an imaginary couple ■ To show awareness of the relationships and emotions involved ■ To demonstrate creativity in designing a suitable programme ■ To work well in a team to produce a coherent outcome	■ Create a programme for the wedding ■ Members of the group can complete chosen activities from sheet ■ Produce a PowerPoint presentation summarising each aspect of the wedding plan ■ Produce a budget spreadsheet for the wedding	Thinking, learning and social skills Literacy Personal and emotional skills Teamwork	En3 Ma4,1c, d, e, f, g Ma4, 2c Ma2, 1b ICT 2a ICT 3b

Activity number	Activity overview	Learning objectives	Possible outcomes	Essentials for learning and life	Some examples of KS2 National Curriculum Programmes of Study covered
3 Estimated time 6 hours	Investigate how weddings can lead to happy family life Look at the role of parents and what makes a good parent Create a leaflet that gives guidance on parenting skills that can be distributed at weddings	■ To consider the challenges of parenting in modern family life ■ To evaluate various types of parenting and what guidance could help ensure success ■ To summarise the above idea and produce useful messages in a variety of forms	■ Discussion on aspects of family life such as discipline, eating, outings, etc. with written work on 'How my family works' ■ How parents can help with feelings (e.g. self-confidence, motivation) ■ Produce a leaflet or website that offers the best advice on being a great parent ■ Local health visitor or nurse can talk about baby health ■ Interviewing parents roleplay ■ Talk from chef or school food manager to produce a menu for a children's healthy wedding dinner	Literacy Fluency ICT Social skills SEAL	Sc2, 2b PSHE/Cit 3a PSHE/Cit 4c
4 Estimated time 3 hours	Wedding exhibition – this is an opportunity to hold an exhibition to show the work that has been done on this project	■ To demonstrate learning about weddings ■ To communicate to other students, parents, etc.	■ Teams can run various stalls including parenting skills, wedding menus, examples of the best wedding plans ■ Fashion shows can be included with wedding dresses from different cultures modelled	Communication skills Teamwork	En1 En3 ICT 1a, b, c ICT 3b ICT 4a, b, c

THE WEDDING PLAN – YOUR TEAM CAN CHOOSE WHICH TASKS TO DO:

Choose which tasks you want to do and who will complete them.

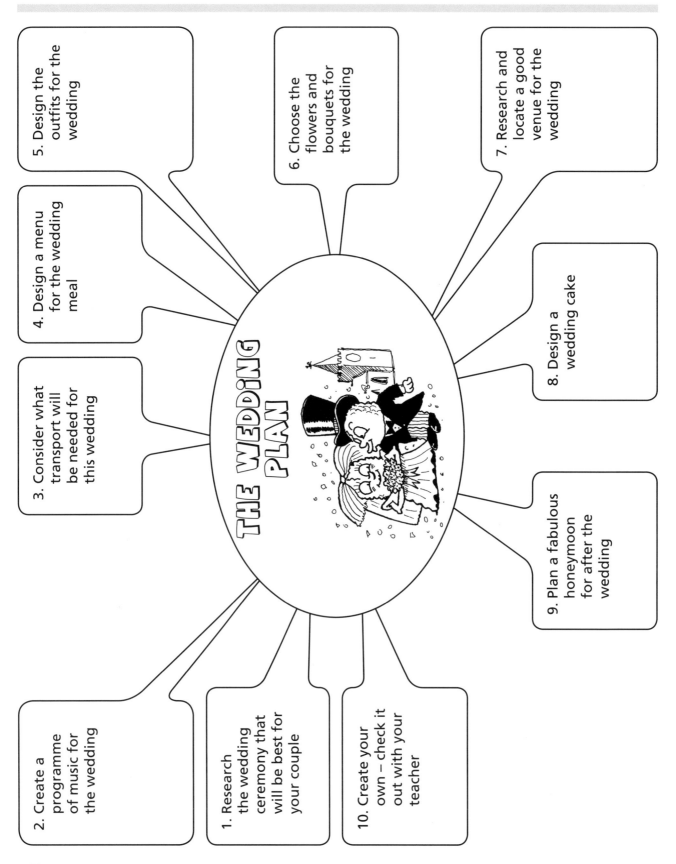

THE WEDDING PLAN

5. Design the outfits for the wedding

4. Design a menu for the wedding meal

3. Consider what transport will be needed for this wedding

6. Choose the flowers and bouquets for the wedding

7. Research and locate a good venue for the wedding

8. Design a wedding cake

9. Plan a fabulous honeymoon for after the wedding

2. Create a programme of music for the wedding

1. Research the wedding ceremony that will be best for your couple

10. Create your own – check it out with your teacher

Example of Wedding Planning programme

Additional columns can be added for transport, honeymoon, outfits, etc. if required.

Venue	Type of ceremony	Number of guests/ special needs	Time and order of events	Food/refreshments	Music/ Entertainment
Whittlebury Hall Arrival in bar Main reception lounge Lotus Room Ballroom	Civil service led by registrar	75 for the day 110 for the evening One wheelchair user One blind guest with guide dog 5 x vegetarian 3 x nut intolerance for evening 1 x wheat allergy	Guests arrive from 12 p.m. Ceremony at 12.30 p.m. Wedding breakfast/ sit down meal at 1.30 p.m. Finger buffet at 9 p.m. Bride and groom leave at 10.30 p.m.	**Nibbles:** Crisps and vegetables **Wedding Breakfast:** *Starter* Mint and pea soup with walnut bread or rye bread *Main course* Lamb shank with redcurrant jus or Red mullet baked in white wine Broccoli and peas Carrot and swede crush *Dessert* Chocolate profiteroles or Lemon tart with raspberry coulis	Background classical String quartet playing 'Perfect Day' as couple walk up the aisle Steel pans band play 'Congratulations' as couple leave reception lounge for Lotus Room Guitarist plays folk tunes during meal Disco from 7.30–9.30 p.m. Rock band playing 9.30–11 p.m.

Venue	Type of ceremony	Number of guests/ special needs	Time and order of events	Food/refreshments	Music/ Entertainment
				Finger buffet: Sausage rolls Salmon sandwiches Cheese and pineapple Vol-au-vents Prawn kebabs Parma ham and melon Fresh fruit Mini cream cakes	

Disaster

Project title and introduction	**DISASTER**
	This project includes elements of the scientific/technological understanding area of learning and geographical understanding through a study of disasters. It also includes opportunities to consider survival which links into the Learning Habits Toolkit.

Activity number	Activity overview	Learning objectives	Possible outcomes	Essentials for learning and life	Some examples of KS2 National Curriculum Programmes of Study covered
1 Estimated time 5 hours	Investigate what disasters are likely in the UK and in other countries and how we react to them Start by researching: Tsunamis (tidal waves) 9/11 Floods Airline crashes Epidemics Volcanic eruptions Nuclear bomb (Nagasaki) Nuclear reactor accident (Chernobyl) Chemical leak (Bhopal)	■ To investigate over time and place what a 'disaster' is and how we respond ■ To consider how we respond to disasters by studying one incident in detail ■ To learn about the possible causes of natural and man-made disasters	■ Watch footage, collect news stories and sources of information about man-made and natural disasters ■ Produce more detailed work on one incident individually or in pairs ■ Extension work: to organise a survey to discover real life stories of disasters by survivors	Literacy/ICT	Ge 1d Ge 4b En2 En3

Activity number	Activity overview	Learning objectives	Possible outcomes	Essentials for learning and life	Some examples of KS2 National Curriculum Programmes of Study covered
2 Estimated time 4 hours	The causes of 'disasters' Choose two of the disasters on the activity sheet, one man-made and one natural, to investigate the causes in more depth Present your findings to the class	■ To discover the processes which result in natural disasters ■ To investigate man's impact on the planet and how it can result in disasters	■ Produce a case study of two examples of real disasters ■ Write a news report about one of the disasters ■ Deliver a talk to the class about one of the disasters	Thinking, learning and social skills Literacy Personal and emotional skills Teamwork	En2 En3
3 Estimated time 8 hours	The survivors What qualities do survivors have? Examine some survival stories Design and prepare an artefact that could be used for survival purposes	■ To explore how humans survive disasters ■ To consider a number of artefacts for survival after a disaster ■ To design ideas for artefacts using CAD ■ To create an artefact	■ Write a story of survival after a disaster ■ Produce an ideas list for survival artefacts ■ Research how to make artefacts ■ Design an artefact and redraft design following feedback from peers and teacher ■ Create the artefact	Literacy Fluency ICT Social skills Teambuilding skills Constructive support and feedback	En1 En2 En3 DT 1 DT 2 DT 3 DT 4
4 Estimated time 3 hours	Exhibition To make an exhibition of the survival artefacts and present them to visitors	■ To present and explain the artefacts, how they work and what their purpose is	■ The exhibition will be open for parents and visitors with children manning the stalls and exhibits	Communication skills Teamwork	En1 Ar 1c, 2a

DISASTER – YOU CAN CHOOSE WHICH THREE TO STUDY:

Natural and man-made disasters.

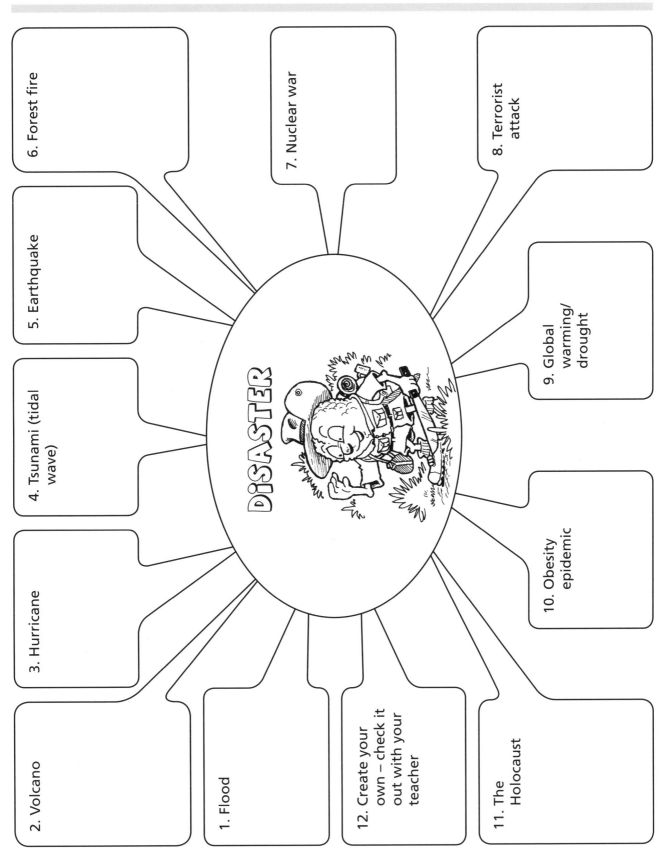

DISASTER

6. Forest fire

7. Nuclear war

8. Terrorist attack

5. Earthquake

9. Global warming/ drought

4. Tsunami (tidal wave)

10. Obesity epidemic

3. Hurricane

2. Volcano

1. Flood

12. Create your own – check it out with your teacher

11. The Holocaust

Disaster – Survival artefact proposal

Disaster environment	Needs of community	Plan to create artefact/survival kit
Flood	Transport	
Artefact ideas	**How it will meet needs**	
Boat		

International Restaurant

Project title and introduction	INTERNATIONAL RESTAURANT
	In this project learners will be investigating the world of catering and culture through creating a restaurant with an international theme. It is an opportunity to link in the science of food and digestion, the foreign languages aspect of the areas of learning and address health and well-being issues by applying learning to a service industry. It also offers an opportunity to bring in local chefs or restaurant proprietors for demonstrations and introduces the notion of good customer service, which links into communication skills.

Activity number	Activity overview	Learning objectives	Possible outcomes	Essentials for learning and life/ competencies	Some examples of KS2 National Curriculum Programmes of Study covered
1 Estimated time 4 hours	Consider food in schools and recent changes in provision Listen to a talk from the school catering manager about how s/he buys food and decides on menus Research different types of restaurants visited. Evaluate styles and quality Teach content on: food safety, healthy diet, digestion, cooking and non-reversible reactions	■ To consider reasons for changes in school food provision in recent years and its impact ■ To know the importance of healthy eating ■ To investigate styles of restaurant and make judgements about preference ■ To evaluate different types of service and how they make customers feel ■ To know the science behind safe, healthy food and its preservation, cooking and digestion	■ Interview students about food provision at school and how it has changed ■ Produce a brochure for your school canteen ■ Classify different types of eating experience (e.g. McDonalds through to silver service) ■ Survey of local restaurants – produce simple graphs to show opinions ■ Roleplay of customer experience – good and bad ■ Prepare healthy food menus, balanced diet posters, etc. ■ Extension work: research in your community about eating out habits	Literacy/ICT SEAL Numeracy	Sc2,1a Sc2, 2b Sc2, 5a, b, f PSHE/Cit 3a, b, g PsHE/Cit 4b, h

Activity number	Activity overview	Learning objectives	Possible outcomes	Essentials for learning and life/ competencies	Some examples of KS2 National Curriculum Programmes of Study covered
2 Estimated time 6 hours	Investigate eating out across the world and why Chinese, Thai, Indian, French, Italian, Greek, etc. restaurants have become commonplace in Britain Undertake detailed research on one type of foreign inspired restaurant (e.g. roles of employees, cost of meals, decor, entertainment) Develop a knowledge of the vocabulary for your chosen restaurant	■ To develop a knowledge of international restaurants and how they function ■ To learn some useful vocabulary to use in a real situation ■ To know that the work of a restaurant is varied and involves a range of tasks	■ Engage a local foreign restaurateur to talk about his/her business ■ Gather some menus from foreign restaurants to compare language ■ Produce a mini study of the chosen restaurant – a picture/photo, typical menu with prices, staff employed, review ■ Trip to a local restaurant ■ Learn some useful foreign language phrases for food and service (e.g. What would you like to eat?). Practice using roleplay ■ Explore table manners and etiquette	Thinking, learning and social skills Literacy Personal and emotional skills Social skills	PSHE/Cit 1e MFL 1d, e, f, g MFL 2a, b, c MFL 3d
3 Estimated time 8 hours	In a team develop your own international restaurant Assign tasks to team members (see sample lesson plan) Present restaurant ideas to each other	■ To work as a team to create an international restaurant	■ Complete task plan for the collaborative worksheet ■ Set success criteria and timescales for each aspect of the project ■ Members of group complete various tasks ■ Cook some sample foods to bring in for the International Food Fair	Literacy Teamwork ICT Social skills	En1 En2 En3

Activity number	Activity overview	Learning objectives	Possible outcomes	Essentials for learning and life/ competencies	Some examples of KS2 National Curriculum Programmes of Study covered
4 Estimated time 3 hours	Demonstrate the restaurants with an International Food Fair Each group sets up a place setting and provides sample foods to represent their restaurant	■ To demonstrate the learning ■ To communicate to other students, parents, etc.	■ Parents and other students can attend the International Food Fair ■ Judges from the local community can present various awards	Communication skills Teamwork	DT (various) PSHE 3a, b

INTERNATIONAL RESTAURANT - CHOOSE YOUR CUISINE:

Choose which tasks you want to do and who will complete them.

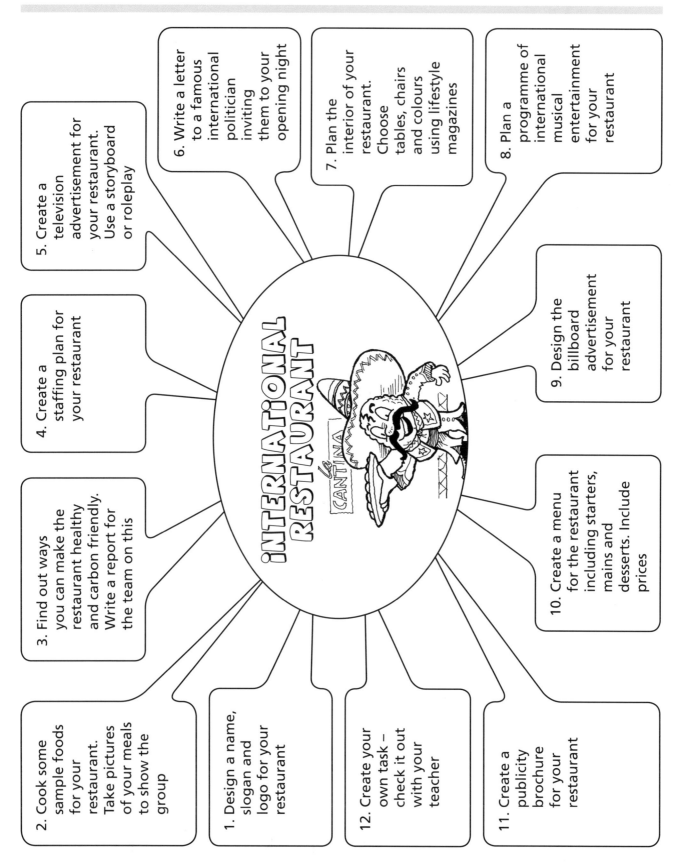

5. Create a television advertisement for your restaurant. Use a storyboard or roleplay

6. Write a letter to a famous international politician inviting them to your opening night

7. Plan the interior of your restaurant. Choose tables, chairs and colours using lifestyle magazines

8. Plan a programme of international musical entertainment for your restaurant

4. Create a staffing plan for your restaurant

INTERNATIONAL RESTAURANT

9. Design the billboard advertisement for your restaurant

3. Find out ways you can make the restaurant healthy and carbon friendly. Write a report for the team on this

10. Create a menu for the restaurant including starters, mains and desserts. Include prices

2. Cook some sample foods for your restaurant. Take pictures of your meals to show the group

1. Design a name, slogan and logo for your restaurant

12. Create your own task – check it out with your teacher

11. Create a publicity brochure for your restaurant

International Restaurant: Sample lesson plan

Starter

Show pictures of various restaurants with an international theme. Play inspiring international music as they enter the classroom.

Thunk: Is a fish and chip shop an international restaurant? (See www.independentthinking.co.uk/ Cool+Stuff/Thunks/default.aspx)

Lesson objectives

Complete task sheet to assign tasks in team.

Competency objectives

Develop awareness of success criteria.

Develop teamworking skills.

Main activity

Introduce task to the students, group discussion – allow for questions.

Groups discuss name and type of restaurant they will work on (10 min.)

Understanding success criteria – how can we set high standards?

Sample activity

All students design a logo for their restaurant (10 min.)

In teams: Discuss success criteria. What are we looking for? List the criteria for a good logo. Choose the best logo and decide what makes it the best (e.g. colourful, eye-catching, stylish, contains a message).

Choose a team captain – discuss methods for this.

Groups plan tasks and assign jobs and complete planning sheet (20 min.)

Plenary

Return to objectives: Is the sheet completed?

What makes good work for the team? (on sticky notes)

Assess how you have performed in the group today? (10 min.)

International Restaurant: Sample lesson plan

International Restaurant task sheet

Team ....

Task number	Who is responsible?	Success criteria: How will we know it's good?	Essential competences	Completed
1	The team agrees the name and logo

Jenny and Jim to do Task 1 and design them on computer | The logo is colourful and eye-catching and has a message which fits in with the brand of the restaurant

The slogan fits well with the logo and gives a good message about the food and service

You have checked out with at least six people their opinion of your slogan and logo | Teamwork

ICT | |
| | | | | |

Task number	Who is responsible?	Success criteria: How will we know it's good?	Essential competences	Completed

Task number	Who is responsible?	Success criteria: How will we know it's good?	Essential competences	Completed

Time Machine

Project title and introduction	
	TIME MACHINE This project begins with learning about how light and sound travel and then develops the science facts into science fiction. Learners will be using the concept of a time machine to investigate life and culture through the ages and to learn about the skills of well-known heroic characters in history. This project provides an opportunity to link historical and social understanding to the essential skills for learning, and tap into aspects of scientific and technological understanding as the learners investigate the influence of great people from the past. This can link to the personal development of the learners as they conclude that the qualities that helped historical characters make an impact can be nurtured in their own lives.

Activity number	Activity overview	Learning objectives	Possible outcomes	Essentials for learning and life/ competencies	Some examples of KS2 National Curriculum Programmes of Study covered
1 Estimated time 4 hours	Consider whether time travel is possible Investigate how light and sound travel Discuss thunder and lightning Discuss science fiction and its relationship to science fact Watch *Dr Who* and the TARDIS considering this as an example of science fiction	■ To know how light and sound travel ■ To use this knowledge to understand the concept of time travel ■ To consider how exciting ideas create science fiction fantasies ■ To evaluate an example of televised science fiction drama that includes a time machine	■ Practical experiments measuring how light and sound travel with explanations and/or recorded data in graphical format ■ Research into shadows and supersonic travel ■ Discussion on science fiction in books and film (e.g. *Dr Who vs. Apollo 13*) ■ Community of Enquiry circle time about the concept of time travel and its implications ■ Extension: study the sky at night. Find out about constellations (e.g. Orion) and how far away the stars in it are. Feedback to the class	Literacy/ICT Numeracy	Sc1 En1 En2 En3

Activity number	Activity overview	Learning objectives	Possible outcomes	Essentials for learning and life/ competencies	Some examples of KS2 National Curriculum Programmes of Study covered
2 Estimated time 4 hours	Design your time machine In groups you will draw, use CAD/CAM to design or make out of waste materials a prototype of your time machine	■ To apply some knowledge and imagination in a collaborative design task ■ To decide together the format and success criteria for the machine ■ To be able to describe the time machine and how it may function ■ To evaluate the work of others from an aesthetic and practical viewpoint	■ PMI (plus minus and interesting bits) the Doctor's TARDIS ■ Set success criteria for your group's time machine ■ Draft sketches and functions of the time machine ■ Create a name for the time machine ■ Produce a written description of the functions of the time machine to accompany a presentation to the rest of the class ■ To evaluate each other's time machines	Thinking skills Social skills ICT Numeracy Literacy	DT (various) En1

Activity number	Activity overview	Learning objectives	Possible outcomes	Essentials for learning and life/ competencies	Some examples of KS2 National Curriculum Programmes of Study covered
3 Estimated time 6 hours	Discover a hero in time Travel back in time in your machine. Your challenge is to learn as much as possible about making a big difference in the world from famous historical characters Sample events and their impact can be investigated – then the team can choose their character from the activity sheet	■ To understand the chronology and impact of important historical events and people ■ To be able to describe what leadership is and how it can impact on society ■ To present in a roleplay or other presentation a profile of the historical event and character which demonstrates their impact on society	■ Draw up a timeline of the historical leaders for the past 1,000 years (local, UK or international) ■ Produce a research project using various sources, retrieving information and reworking it as evidence to present to the class about the chosen hero ■ Performance of roleplay with time machine and travel back to a famous event ■ Letter from chosen famous character explaining how s/he motivated him/herself and what s/he achieved ■ Debate/hotseating using the chosen characters from history ■ Evaluate each other's presentations	Literacy Teamwork ICT Social skills	Hi 1a, b Hi 13 Hi 4b En3 En1

Activity number	Activity overview	Learning objectives	Possible outcomes	Essentials for learning and life/ competencies	Some examples of KS2 National Curriculum Programmes of Study covered
4

Estimated time

3 hours | Present an assembly to the rest of the school showing the favourite characters from the above activity

Demonstrate what you have learned from the heroes of the past and make a hall display that will help everyone in school to remember them | ■ To communicate to other students what we can learn from historical heroes who made an impact on the world | ■ List of heroic qualities (e.g. courage, determination, communication skills) displayed in school and children rewarded for showing evidence of these traits | Communication skills

Teamwork

SEAL | Hi 1a, b
En1
En3
ICT 1b
ICT 3b |

The Time Machine fact sheet

Light and sound

Sound travels at 340 metres per second (340 m/s) in air. This equals 1,236 kilometres per hour (768 mph) or about one kilometre in three seconds (and about one mile in five seconds).

Light travels at 300,000,000 m/s or 300 million m/s. This equals just over 1 billion km/hour (about 671 million miles/h), or about 300,000 kilometres/s (186,000 miles/s.)

We see objects because light bounces off them into our eyes. Because light travels so fast it takes next to no time at all for light to travel from the person you are talking to into your eyes. Also because the person is close (let's say one metre away) the sounds they make also seem to travel more or less instantly to your ears. (Their speech takes only 1/340th of a second to reach you.)

Thunder and lightning

When a hot lightning bolt sizzles down through the air, it heats up the air so much that it glows white hot. This obviously gives off light which travels to our eyes. The very hot air in a lightning bolt expands massively, pushing away colder air around it and causing the thunder we hear.

Imagine that a lightning bolt came down one kilometre away from you. The light would travel even this distance (1,000 m) almost instantly – remember it travels at 300 million m/s. But the sound only travels at 340 m/s. So it would take 1,000/340 = 2.9 s to reach you. You can work out how far away lightning is by counting these numbers out loud, fairly slowly – 1,001 … 1,002 … 1,003 … It takes about a second to say each one. So if you count up to 1,006 the lightning is two kilometres away.

Seeing stars (and travelling in time)

Now think about stars in the sky – they are like our sun, only very far away. Light from them travels (at the speed of light, of course) through space into our eyes. The nearest star to us is called Proxima Centauri. It is so far away that even light takes over four years to reach us. So when we see this star, we are looking at light that set off from this star four years ago. We are looking back in time.

Now imagine that we have a really powerful telescope on Earth and Bobby points it at Proxima Centauri. The telescope captures light from Proxima Centauri as it was four years ago. Then Bobby notices that there is a planet orbiting the star. He zooms in and can see the surface. He zooms in further and can see cities and then finally Bobby zooms in enough to see aliens walking around. What Bobby is seeing happened four years ago. Has Bobby become a time traveller?

What if Bobby saw another alien looking straight back at him through an alien telescope. Could Bobby and the alien communicate by flashing lights at each other? How long would it take to send and receive a message? If Bobby wants to have a normal conversation the signals he sends and receives would have to travel faster than light. Scientists say this is not possible – nothing travels faster than light.

And this is Proxima Centauri – some stars we see in the sky are millions of light years away! We see them as they were millions of years ago.

Finally, imagine that Bobby builds a spaceship to travel to Proxima Centauri. The spaceship can travel much faster than light, so he makes the journey instantly. Bobby has a 10 minute chat with the friendly alien with the telescope, says goodbye and goes instantly back to Earth. Four years later Bobby uses his telescope on Earth and points it at the spot where he and the alien had their chat. What does Bobby see? Does this mean Bobby went forward in time? Is Bobby's spaceship a time machine?

THE TIME MACHINE – CHOOSE YOUR HISTORICAL HERO:

Produce a dossier on your chosen character: where they lived, what they looked like, what they achieved, why they are important, what other people have said about them and why you have chosen them.

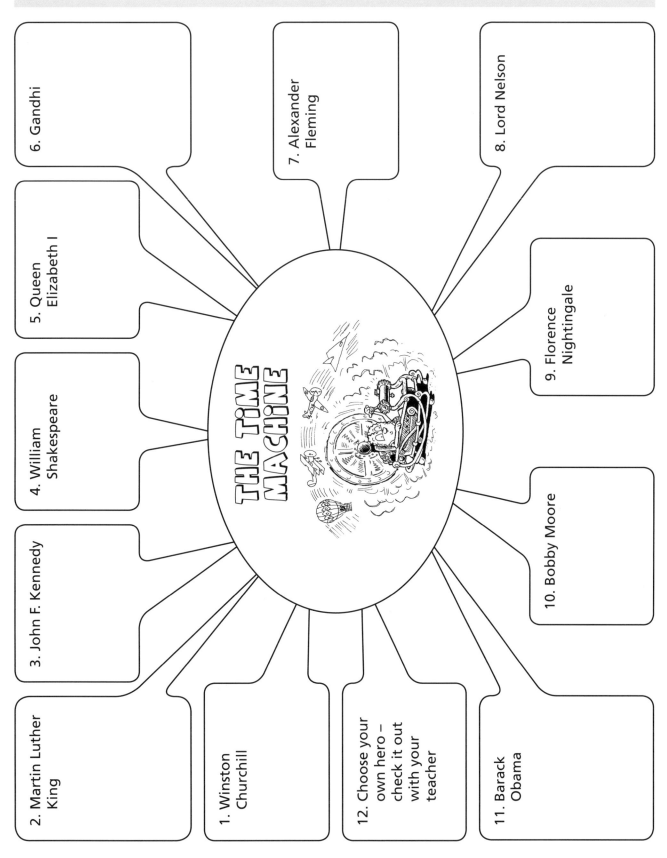

6. Gandhi

7. Alexander Fleming

8. Lord Nelson

5. Queen Elizabeth I

4. William Shakespeare

9. Florence Nightingale

3. John F. Kennedy

THE TIME MACHINE

2. Martin Luther King

1. Winston Churchill

12. Choose your own hero – check it out with your teacher

11. Barack Obama

10. Bobby Moore

Section III
The Stories

- Implementing a creative curriculum through cross-curricular projects
- Developing social and emotional intelligence
- Creating independent, confident and lifelong learners

Introduction

The three stories in this section can be read to the class to give an insight into how the personal and social skills can be put into practice in real life. Bobby's adventures in these three stories provide an extended metaphor for the application of gumption, learning to learn and great communication skills. They can be used in between projects or within literacy lessons. They can also be used to inspire children to write their own stories about Bobby's adventures

The Magic Carpet

It was raining outside and Bobby was bored. Everyone at home had gone shopping and all his friends were at Jasper's party. 'It's not fair,' thought Bobby as he kicked the big beanbag in his bedroom and threw himself onto the bed, rolling himself up in his duvet. He closed his eyes and shouted out loud enough for anyone to hear: 'I wish I was anywhere but here in this boring house in this boring village in this boring country.'

As he said it, he tumbled off the bed with the duvet wrapped around him onto the Persian carpet on the floor and moaned and groaned some more. He forced some fake tears out of his big blue eyes and started blubbing with self-pity, when something suddenly took his breath away. Beneath him the carpet seemed to move. It rumbled and shook and bounced him about before raising him up in a jerky motion that practically threw him through the air.

'Yikes,' he cried, hanging onto the edge of the carpet in fear of his life. He looked down and realised he was a metre off the floor and swaying in the wind … but he couldn't be! He was in his bedroom! Looking out the window from this height he could see the tree tops and realised he was floating on air – no not on air, on his carpet, *in* the air! Now this was fun, it must be some kind of levitation but he was definitely hovering. He reached over to the window and balancing carefully he unhooked the latch and swung it open. A chilly blast of air whipped in through the window and seemed to sweep around the room and under his magic carpet. With a sudden lurch the carpet launched itself out of the window with Bobby hanging onto the sides, his little legs dangling off the front and his mouth wide open.

Outside it was cold and damp and Bobby used his duvet to shield himself from the rain and wind as he flew on his magic carpet through the trees. But as it picked up speed, the duvet ballooned and hit a branch. Bobby hung on bravely as the carpet flew on through the storm, tipping him from one side to the other as it rose above the trees higher and higher. He dared to glance down and saw his home get smaller and smaller. He felt scared and cold as he soared through the air. His hands were aching and frozen and he was slipping off the carpet. 'Stop,' he yelled. 'Please stop, slow down. Where are we going? I want to go home …' He sobbed and shuffled his bottom back to the middle of the carpet. He looked up and saw a huge white owl flying alongside him with its wings outstretched. When it turned its head towards Bobby he saw its huge yellow eyes and hooked black beak. 'Climb on my back, Bobby,' said the bird. 'Stop sniffling and I will show you some magic.'

Bobby was terrified: 'I can't even stay on this mad carpet. How can I get on your back? I'm scared, please take me home.'

The snowy owl flew closer and started singing a favourite song of Bobby's in a strange sweet voice – a song that made him feel brave and strong. Bobby started mouthing the words and as he did so the carpet seemed to stabilise and the rain became softer. The owl's wing came close to the carpet and Bobby sang louder until the song filled the air and made him brave enough to shuffle across the wing and onto the bird's soft back. 'Yippee!' he cried as they veered off towards a patch of blue sky. Meanwhile the carpet appeared to head off back home.

Bobby sat astride the bird's back and started to enjoy the ride until the owl said, 'Hold on tight, we're going down.' He swooped down and Bobby gasped as they cut through trees and houses towards an island in the middle of a large lake before coming to land on a grassy bank beside a rocky cliff. Bobby slipped off the owl's back and landed with his feet in the air. Before he could stand up the owl had flown away and Bobby was alone staring at a cave in front of him and feeling terribly afraid once again.

No one came to his rescue so Bobby picked himself up and went to explore. He peered inside the cavern and stepped into the shelter of the rocky outcrop. He edged in deeper into the darkness. He could smell damp and a faint aroma of rotting flesh. He had to step around puddles of stagnant liquid but something made him keep moving forward, deeper and deeper into the cave. He crouched down below a craggy rock and crawled into a narrow passage with water trickling down the wall into a stream at the bottom. As he stepped around the corner there was an old sleeping bag scrunched up on the ground, as if someone had been camping out there. Bobby could hear his own heart beating with terror as he heard a noise behind him. Something was there. In the darkness. It was moving towards him. He froze.

A flap of white wings seemed to light up the cave and Bobby felt a gentle breeze as the huge snowy owl swept past his head. Bobby wanted to turn and run and run until he got away but suddenly he saw the bird's two huge staring golden eyes which fixed him to the spot. The eyes were staring past him and he followed their gaze to a small hole in the cave wall where something glinted in the darkness. Bobby reached for the shiny object and pulled it towards him. It was a battered bronze lantern in the shape of a gravy boat. The snowy owl blinked slowly and said in a lovely, calm, deep voice: 'Now, you have the secret magic, the magic secret.' Then, with a gentle flap of its enormous wings it was off and away.

'Wait for me,' said Bobby. 'Tell me what to do … please … wait …' But the owl was gone.

Bobby suddenly felt very alone and lost. It was cold and dark and he was a long way from home. He tucked the lantern under his arm and tried to run back the way he had come. It was slippery and craggy and now he wasn't sure which way to go. Was it getting darker? It seemed so much further than when he had come in. Where was the entrance? He stood still and looked for light … but he was trapped. It was gloomy and wet and he couldn't find his way out. He leaned against the wall sobbing and exhausted when he saw some big letters carved into the rock: 'Today is the first day of the rest of your life.'

Bobby sat and wiped the dirt and tears from his face and looked at the dull bronze of his lantern. On the side were some scratched the initials 'BB'. He rubbed them to see properly and as he did something very strange occurred.

A wispy stream of smoke appeared from the spout of the lantern and seemed to create a cloud above Bobby's head. In the haze he could see the words, 'Follow the light and the compass in your head. Keep calm and just keep going.' Bobby breathed deeply, then from nowhere he heard the same song he had sung with the owl when they were flying through the air. He hummed it softly to himself and started moving slowly and more confidently along the tunnel. Then, at last, he saw streaks of light on the cave wall. He followed them calmly and steadily, still humming his song, and he breathed deeply as the tunnel got lighter and lighter.

At the cave entrance he smiled and noticed the sun had lightened the sky and he was not far from the mainland. He needed to swim across. Bobby thought quickly, then grabbed some reeds to strap the lantern to his back, waded into the water and swam the short distance to the shore. He tramped ashore, wet and shivery, but feeling brave and determined. Shaking himself off, he strode out inland towards a public footpath sign. He felt calm and resolute and decided to get himself home – his parents would be wondering where he had got to. Walking quickly along the path he knew he could get home – if he just kept on walking. Reaching some shops and houses Bobby saw familiar sights and asked for directions to his home village.

Two hours later he was back in his own street, sweaty and tired, still clutching his magic lantern. He let himself in the back door and heard the family chatting in the lounge. He dashed upstairs to his bedroom and gasped as he saw the window wide open and banging in the breeze. On the floor was the carpet that had begun his journey, slightly rumpled but good as new. He closed the window quickly and placed the battered lantern deep under his bed.

In the bathroom, he splashed water onto his face and hands and felt happy as he looked in the mirror and thought about his adventure and his magic lantern. Then, with a wide smile on his face, he ran downstairs to join the others, humming his special song and shouting, 'Hello, you lot, what have you been buying?' Bobby was glowing with secret confidence after his mysterious adventure … and he knew he would be using that shiny lantern and its magic genius again sometime very soon!

The Reptile, the Rabbit and the Snowy Owl

Bobby woke up early. It was snowing and the whole of his garden was covered with a beautiful wintry blanket. He jumped out of bed and pulled on some warm woollies, ready for going out to investigate. After breakfast the doorbell chimed and three of his friends were waiting for him on the step. As the four little figures tramped across the white drive in their wellies, they kicked up the snow at each other and enjoyed making the first footprints in the pristine path.

Bobby skidded along behind his mates opening his mouth to catch the flakes falling on his face. Suddenly a big lump of snow hit his head and knocked him over. He slipped and skidded and fell flat on his bottom. He heard his friends laughing as he looked up through teary eyes, wiping the snow from his face.

'That hurt!' he shouted. 'Who did it?' he sobbed, as he rubbed his sore backside and got to his feet.

'Only messing,' said one of his friends. 'You should see your face – its soooo funny!'

Suddenly, inside Bobby's head a huge angry reptile appeared, snarling and thrashing around. It looked like a cross between a crocodile, a Tyrannosaurus Rex and a fire-breathing dragon and it was roaring inside his mind: 'They're laughing at you! You have to get them back … go on … make them pay!'

Bobby saw red. He felt the blood rush to his brain and his heart started beating extra fast. He didn't think about it, he just ran at one of his mates and rugby-tackled him to the ground. Suddenly he was sitting on top of him and had his hands round his neck pressing hard. The others came over and tried to pull Bobby off. He hit back. Scooping up some snow and stones he threw it at them, sobbing and screaming and kicking out as they dragged him off his friend.

'What is it with you, Bobby? Calm down. You're mad, you are!' His friends were scared.

'I will not calm down, I will not! I hate you! I'm gonna kill you all!' He lashed out viciously, half crying, half shouting.

The others ran off afraid and left Bobby in a heap on the ground, sobbing uncontrollably and feeling very sorry for himself. The reptile in his head was still whirling around, growling and smirking as Bobby kicked and cried in frustration. Left alone in the lane, he got colder and colder and felt very alone.

When he opened his eyes he saw something wonderful. Perched on the fence a metre away was a beautiful snowy white owl with piercing amber eyes. Looking serene and calm, the owl cooed at Bobby: 'Don't let that evil dragon take hold of your thinking. Laugh at your mistakes, joke about yourself. Know that you can keep calm in any crisis. It will make you stronger, Bobby.' And then it took off in a snowy flurry, leaving Bobby wondering if it was ever there.

Bobby felt different. Definitely calmer, but still hurt and sad. And wet and cold. He stood up and wiped the snow off himself. He felt ashamed of how he had behaved. He hoped he hadn't lost his friends forever. He knew the owl was right and he should have joked along when he fell over, no matter how embarrassed he was.

He wandered along the lane, not really knowing where he was going. The joy of the day had disappeared and now he was alone. After an hour or so he found his way back home and sneaked upstairs to his bedroom ignoring his mum's questions. As he lay on his bed feeling sad and sulky, he suddenly remembered the magic lantern under his bed. He pulled it out and looked at it. He rubbed the dirt from the faint initials 'BB' and suddenly the room filled with a cloudy dust and the lovely fragrant smell of lemons. The cloud seemed to sit above his head and helped him to think clearly about what had happened. 'I am never going to lose my temper like that again,' Bobby thought. 'I behaved like an idiot, I lost control – it was horrible and I don't have to do it. I need to learn to get some thinking tips. Mmm … How and where?'

Bobby looked around his room and suddenly he saw it … sitting very still in the corner. It was a giant floppy eared rabbit, white with pink ears and soft fur, nearly as big as Bobby himself. He shot towards it, stroking its velvety coat. 'Where have you come from? You are gorgeous, so soft, so fluffy, so sweet.' As Bobby stroked the rabbit he immediately felt happier. The rabbit looked up appreciatively, making small noises like a happy cat. Bobby snuggled his face up against the long silky ears, feeling completely safe. He closed his eyes and heard a distant sound of singing. It was the song he had sung with the owl that made him feel good and brave and proud. It seemed to be coming from the rabbit and as Bobby looked carefully at the rabbit's eyes he knew what it was thinking.

'Use this music to be brave and strong when you need to be. Make up a rhyme to remind you to take responsibility. Use pictures and mind movies to help you create great memories. Make sure you try to understand your emotions and know you can control them and use them in a positive way. Remember, if you think you can, you can – it's all about learning. Now, create a picture in your head. Make it colourful and exciting. See your friends and you playing in the snow and having fun. You get hit by a snowball and you laugh, you fall over and you smile …'

And Bobby could see the picture! He started smiling to himself. He knew just what to do! First he ran downstairs and got the biggest, juiciest carrot he could find to give to the rabbit. But when he got back to his room it had gone.

Still smiling and remembering the rabbit's advice, Bobby rushed to get his warm clothes on again and was soon out in the street. He looked everywhere for his friends and finally saw them building a snowman on the village green. He stood for a moment watching and wondering how he could help and make it up to his friends when he suddenly discovered he still had the carrot in his pocket. That was it!

'Hey you lot!' Bobby shouted. 'What are you doing?' He ran over to them and said, 'I'm so sorry about before. I was being stupid and it won't happen again. Here's a nose for your snowman!'

And Bobby reached into his pocket and pulled out the carrot and stuck it onto the snowman. It made a fabulous nose. It looked so strange that all the friends fell about together laughing.

Prince Charming and the Gumption Tree

At last it was the day that Bobby was to go to Buckingham Palace. He had been planning it for weeks and still couldn't believe he was going to be given a special award, the MCC – Master of Charming Communication – by the Queen. He had earned this award by helping out in the community, raising money for charity and making people feel good by having lovely manners and being kind and polite. He had bought a great new outfit with a bow-tie and a special stretch limo was coming to pick him up to take him to the palace.

He had decided to take his friend Frankie with him to the ceremony. All his friends and his mum, of course, wanted to go but Bobby chose Frankie because he was always so cool and smart and Bobby wanted to impress him and get to be his best friend. He hoped that one day he could convince Frankie also to be polite and charming, but this was going to be a challenge. The two friends felt really important as the limousine cruised through the streets and people stopped to stare. Frankie kept leaning out of the car and shouting things, which was a bit embarrassing. Bobby also felt disappointed that Frankie had his old trainers on when Bobby had taken ages polishing his shiny red shoes.

When Bobby arrived at the palace, the car took him through the huge gates with the smart soldiers standing in their red jackets and massive bearskin hats. Frankie reached out and prodded one of the guards and called him a nasty name as they went through. He giggled madly as he saw the soldier blush.

'Frankie, don't do that – you're not allowed,' whispered Bobby.

'Lighten up you little brain box!' said Frankie. 'We're here to have some fun!'

The limo pulled up outside two huge pillars which marked the entrance to the palace. As the two friends got out, photographers snapped their pictures and smart people in suits showed them the right way to go. But Frankie ducked down, grabbed Bobby and before he knew it they were running across a courtyard, around the back of the palace and into a backroom.

'Hey Brainy – this is cool – let's find some food,' Frankie said as he slapped the back of Bobby's head.

'But ... but ... but ... what about my award?' pleaded Bobby.

In the corridor Frankie could smell cooking and he set off running and jumping like a mad thing with Bobby trailing behind, trying to get his attention to calm him down. Suddenly Frankie turned round, twisted and tripped over, bashing his head on the marble floor with an almighty crack. He lay very still, bleeding and unconscious.

Bobby was panic stricken. What should he do? He ran out into the palace gardens, anxiously looking for someone to help. No one was around. As he ran past a window he saw the ceremony had started. An orchestra was playing and people were lining up to collect their awards. Bobby felt desperate – he didn't know what to do or where to get help. The scorching sun was burning his head and sweat was bursting from his pores. He had to calm down. Luckily he spotted a lovely shady tree in the middle of the courtyard. When he got close he could see it had tiny pink flowers in the shape of little hearts. As he reached to pull down a bough to smell the scent, the branch seemed to wrap itself around his arm and pull him closer to the tree. The scent surrounded him, making him feel faint and dreamy. Then as he leaned against the knobbly trunk to rest, he heard a voice float through the branches saying, 'You really are going to need some gumption now, my dear.' At the same time Bobby thought he saw the wings of the snowy owl fluttering above him. 'This is the Gumption Tree' the voice said. 'You *will* find the answers ...'

'What can I do?' Bobby pleaded and looked up through the branches. 'It would be *so* rude to interrupt the ceremony to get help for Frankie. I just can't ...'

'Have courage, be persistent, and don't give up until you find a way,' said the tree.

The words came to him as powerfully as the scent of the blossom: 'You need to get help – you need to be brave.' Suddenly Bobby knew what to do. He ran from the tree towards the ceremony room, towards the huge doors guarded by the red-jacketed guards in the big hats.

The soldiers looked confused and barred his way. Bobby had to become an MCC – a Master of Charming Communication – and fast. He also had to use a lot of gumption. 'I'm terribly sorry to bother you, but I have to get help. Please forgive me,' he said politely, as with his mind racing he slipped between them and pushed open the huge door.

He ran down the red carpet in the middle of the ceremony room, not stopping until he reached the platform at the end of the hall. On the platform was a lady with a crown and a lovely white dress and golden robe. In front of her was a figure kneeling with his head bowed. She lifted a sword: 'Oh my goodness,' thought Bobby, 'she's going to chop off his head!'

'Please madam – STOP!' Bobby shouted, and at this moment he turned to see hundreds of faces looking up at him. Five armed guards stepped forward and grabbed Bobby firmly.

Bobby felt brave and told the soldiers, 'I came here to tell you about my friend, he's hurt … Please, he needs help. I'm so sorry for disturbing the ceremony.'

As the soldiers dragged Bobby away he continued to bravely explain what had happened and persisted in calmly asking the soldiers to help Frankie.

'I am so sorry for interrupting. Please, please just help me find my injured friend.' The soldiers looked at Bobby first grimly, then puzzled, then kindly. 'Look son,' said one of them, 'you seem like a trustworthy and smart kid. We will give you one chance before we cart you off to the police station for what could be a very long stay.'

Ten minutes later Frankie was in an ambulance with Bobby sitting beside him. As he regained consciousness he asked Bobby, 'What happened? Are we in the limo?' Bobby smiled but looked sadly at his shiny red shoes and realised he had missed his chance to get his award. Instead he'd had the most embarrassing experience of his life.

Four months later, Bobby was back at the palace, this time lined up in place, ready to get his medal pinned onto his blazer. He was feeling proud and not a bit nervous. As he waited, he looked out of the window into the courtyard at the magic Gumption Tree. He remembered the moment when he stood underneath it in a panic and full of despair but found the calm courage to save his friend. As he looked into the huge audience he saw his mum proudly watching.

He knew he had learnt how to be brave when he needed to be. He bowed to her Majesty with a polite smile as she gave him his MCC – Bobby Brain, Master of Charming Communication. He felt so proud he wanted to burst.

Section IV
Tools for Assessing and Tracking Skills

- Implementing a creative curriculum through cross-curricular projects
- Developing social and emotional intelligence
- Creating independent, confident and lifelong learners

Assessment of learning in the projects

The projects in Section II have an important part to play in developing essential life and learning skills so it may be useful for learners to record their performance. This reflective assessment is aimed at developing a language for learning and a way of improving key skills and self-awareness. It is not designed to judge grades and levels. A useful approach is for learners to self-assess, peer-assess then talk to the teacher about their progress. The purpose of the assessment is to reflect on what skills they need to develop in the next project.

Essentials for learning and for life – the evidence

Evidence for all of these skills can be found in each project apart from in shaded areas. Use this sheet to mark which project will demonstrate each of the essential skills (see example). Then turn to the detailed assessment sheet to reflect on performance. For a tighter focus on Social and Emotional Aspects of Learning (SEAL) skills just reflect on the habits from Section I.

Essential life and learning skills	Bobby's Magic Towers	Exodus	The Wedding Plan	Disaster	International Restaurant	The Time Machine
Literacy Listen and talk Read different texts Write and present in a variety of ways Analyse, evaluate and criticise						
Numeracy Represent and model situations Use numbers and measurements Use data to support decisions						
ICT Find and select information Create, manipulate and process information Collaborate and communicate information						
Learning and thinking Investigate and question Create and generate ideas Use a range of media to communicate Evaluate own and other's work						
Personal and emotional Identify personal strengths Manage feelings Reflect on learning Set goals Work independently Develop control						

Essential life and learning skills	Bobby's Magic Towers	Exodus	The Wedding Plan	Disaster	International Restaurant	The Time Machine
Social skills Show empathy Adapt behaviours Work collaboratively Negotiate and share ideas Give support and feedback						

BOBBY'S MAGIC TOWERS

Look through the work you have produced. Put a cross on these arrows showing how well you feel you performed in each of these skills for this project. Set yourself targets for improvement.

	Poor	Fair	Good	Excellent
Literacy Listen and talk Read different texts Write and present in a variety of ways Analyse, evaluate and criticise				→
ICT Find and select information Create, manipulate and process information Collaborate and communicate information				→
Learning and thinking Investigate and question Create and generate ideas Use a range of media to communicate Evaluate own and other's work				→
Personal and emotional Identify personal strengths Manage feelings Reflect on learning Set goals Work independently Develop control				→
Social skills Show empathy Adapt behaviours Work collaboratively Negotiate and share ideas Give support and feedback				→

Targets for improvement

1. ....

2. ....

3. ....

EXODUS

Put a cross on these arrows showing how well you feel you performed in each of these skills for this project. Set yourself targets for improvement.

	Poor	Fair	Good	Excellent
Literacy Listen and talk Read different texts Write and present in a variety of ways Analyse, evaluate and criticise				→
ICT Find and select information Create, manipulate and process information Collaborate and communicate information				→
Learning and thinking Investigate and question Create and generate ideas Use a range of media to communicate Evaluate own and other's work				→
Personal and emotional Identify personal strengths Manage feelings Reflect on learning Set goals Work independently Develop control				→
Social skills Show empathy Adapt behaviours Work collaboratively Negotiate and share ideas Give support and feedback				→

Targets for improvement

1. ....

2. ....

3. ....

THE WEDDING PLAN

Put a cross on these arrows showing how well you feel you performed in each of these skills for this project. Set yourself targets for improvement.

	Poor	Fair	Good	Excellent
Literacy Listen and talk Read different texts Write and present in a variety of ways Analyse, evaluate and criticise				⟶
Numeracy Represent and model situations Use number and measurements Use data to support decisions				⟶
ICT Find and select information Create, manipulate and process information Collaborate and communicate information				⟶
Learning and thinking Investigate and question Create and generate ideas Use a range of media to communicate Evaluate own and other's work				⟶
Personal and emotional Identify personal strengths Manage feelings Reflect on learning Set goals Work independently Develop control				⟶
Social skills Show empathy Adapt behaviours Work collaboratively Negotiate and share ideas Give support and feedback				⟶

Targets for improvement

1. ....

2. ....

3. ....

DISASTER

Put a cross on these arrows showing how well you feel you performed in each of these skills for this project. Set yourself targets for improvement.

	Poor	Fair	Good	Excellent
Literacy Listen and talk Read different texts Write and present in a variety of ways Analyse, evaluate and criticise				→
Numeracy Represent and model situations Use number and measurements Use data to support decisions				→
ICT Find and select information Create, manipulate and process information Collaborate and communicate information				→
Learning and thinking Investigate and question Create and generate ideas Use a range of media to communicate Evaluate own and other's work				→
Personal and emotional Identify personal strengths Manage feelings Reflect on learning Set goals Work independently Develop control				→
Social skills Show empathy Adapt behaviours Work collaboratively Negotiate and share ideas Give support and feedback				→

Targets for improvement

1. ....

2. ....

3. ....

INTERNATIONAL RESTAURANT

Put a cross on these arrows showing how well you feel you performed in each of these skills for this project. Set yourself targets for improvement.

	Poor	Fair	Good	Excellent
Literacy Listen and talk Read different texts Write and present in a variety of ways Analyse, evaluate and criticise				→
Numeracy Represent and model situations Use number and measurements Use data to support decisions				→
ICT Find and select information Create, manipulate and process information Collaborate and communicate information				→
Learning and thinking Investigate and question Create and generate ideas Use a range of media to communicate Evaluate own and other's work				→
Personal and emotional Identify personal strengths Manage feelings Reflect on learning Set goals Work independently Develop control				→
Social skills Show empathy Adapt behaviours Work collaboratively Negotiate and share ideas Give support and feedback				→

Targets for improvement

1. ....

2. ....

3. ....

THE TIME MACHINE

Put a cross on these arrows showing how well you feel you performed in each of these skills for this project. Set yourself targets for improvement.

	Poor	Fair	Good	Excellent
Literacy Listen and talk Read different texts Write and present in a variety of ways Analyse, evaluate and criticise				→
Numeracy Represent and model situations Use number and measurements Use data to support decisions				→
ICT Find and select information Create, manipulate and process information Collaborate and communicate information				→
Learning and thinking Investigate and question Create and generate ideas Use a range of media to communicate Evaluate own and other's work				→
Personal and emotional Identify personal strengths Manage feelings Reflect on learning Set goals Work independently Develop control				→
Social skills Show empathy Adapt behaviours Work collaboratively Negotiate and share ideas Give support and feedback				→

Targets for improvement

1. ....

2. ....

3. ....

Glossary

APP	Assessment of Pupil Progress. It is intended that these progression models from QCDA will show how students demonstrate the level they have achieved in subjects, in order to provide summative assessment
Assessment for learning	Assessment that contributes to the learning process, usually identified with research by Wiliam and Black
Coaching	Supportive teaching and guiding
Cognitive skills	Another name for thinking skills
Community of Enquiry	Collaborative investigation where group research and interpretation is used as a method of learning
Competency/competences	Clusters of skills, abilities and expertise
Competency-based curriculum	A curriculum that delivers personal, learning and thinking skills as well as knowledge/content in a cross-curricular model
Creative curriculum	A curriculum that is innovative and collaborative as opposed to prescriptive
Digital immigrant	Older generations born before 1980 who have had to learn electronic communication and have more varying degrees of comfort with new technology
Digital native	Children who have grown up with ICT and the internet so are highly skilled and habitually comfortable with electronic communication
Emotional intelligence	The ability to manage thinking and emotions in order to be effective
Empathy	The ability to understand another's viewpoint
Essential life and learning skills	Literacy, numeracy, ICT, learning and thinking, personal and emotional, social skills
Experiential learning	Learning by practical experience
Formative assessment	Assessment that forms part of the learning process and relates to assessment for learning
Gumption	Resourcefulness, determination, resilience
Habits	Regular behaviours and thinking that create certain outcomes
I-learn	The habit that helps children understand their learning skills and preferences
Learning check	A tool to check at the end of each lesson how far children have progressed with their learning
Learning progress	The progress made towards the learning objective in any activity or lesson
Learning styles	Individual methods and modes of learning

Learning to Learn	The term used for programmes of study that teach students about neuroscience and learning styles in order to support their learning skills. See the Campaign for Learning research project directed by Newcastle University
Metacognition	Reflecting on thinking and learning
Mind movies	Visualising positive events and images as a mental rehearsal for future outcomes
Multiple intelligence	A model of intelligence first cited by Howard Gardner that demonstrates cognitive ability in a variety of ways beyond literacy and numeracy
Opening Minds	The Royal Society of Arts (RSA) model for cross-curricular teaching to develop student competences
P4C	Philosophy for Children. Teaching using philosophical questioning and democratic principles
Peer-assessment	Judging the performance of a peer against criteria
Personalised learning	Learning that is matched to the individual needs of the learner
PLTS	The Personal, Learning and Thinking Skills defined by QCDA
SEAL	Social and Emotional Aspects of Learning. A set of resources and guidance provided to improve well-being and performance in schools. See www.bandapilot.org for a range of resources
Self-assessment	Judging ones own performance against criteria
Skills	Usually more practical ability
Summative assessment	Assessment at the end of a course that demonstrates learning
Thinking skills	The term used to describe skills which develop a range of techniques for remembering, extending higher order thinking and creative thinking
Transferrable skills	Abilities and skills that can be transferred from one context to another
Values	The principles that govern behaviours and attitudes
VLE	Virtual Learning Environment. The electronic interactive resources available to support learning
Willpower	Determination and deferred gratification

Bibliography and wider reading

A'Echevarria, A. de. *Thinking through School* (London: Chris Kington, 2006).

Bandler, R. and Fitzpatrick, O. *Conversations: Freedom is Everything and Love is all the Rest* (Dublin: Mysterious Publications, 2005).

Beere, J. *The Learner's Toolkit* (Carmarthen: Crown House, 2007).

Beere, J. and Boyle, H. *The Competency Curriculum Toolkit* (Carmarthen: Crown House, 2009).

Bosher, M. and Hazlewood, P. *Nurturing Independent Thinkers* (Stafford: Network Educational Press, 2006).

Bransford, J. D., Brown, A. L. and Cocking, R. R. (eds.) *How People Learn: Brain, Mind, Experience and School* (Washington, DC: CBASSE, 2000).

Claxton, G. *Hare Brain, Tortoise Mind* (London: Fourth Estate, 1997).

Craig, C. *Creating Confidence* (Glasgow: Centre for Confidence and Well-Being, 2007).

Curran, A. *The Little Book of Big Stuff about the Brain* (Carmarthen: Crown House, 2008).

Hargreaves D. (chair), *About Learning: Report of the Learning Working Group* (London: Demos, 2004).

Duckworth, J. *The Little Book of Values* (Carmarthen: Crown House, 2009).

Friedman, T. L. *The World is Flat: The Globalized World in the Twenty-First Century* (London: Penguin, 2005).

Gardner, H. *Frames of Mind: The Theory of Multiple Intelligence* (London: Montana, 1984).

Gatto, J. T. *Dumbing Us Down: The Hidden Curriculum of Compulsory Schooling* (Philadelphia, PA: New Society Publishers, 2006).

Galliano, J. *Dear Me: A Letter to my Sixteen-Year-Old Self* (London: Simon & Schuster, 2009).

Gilbert, I. *Essential Motivation in the Classroom* (London: Routledge, 2002).

Gilbert, I. *The Little Books of Thunks* (Carmarthen: Crown House, 2007).

Ginnis, S. and Ginnis, P. *Covering the Curriculum with Stories* (Carmarthen: Crown House, 2009).

Gladwell, M. *Outliers: The Story of Success* (London: Penguin, 2008).

Goleman, D. *Emotional Intelligence: Why It Can Matter More Than IQ* (London: Bloomsbury, 1996).

Greenfield, S. *The Private Life of the Brain* (London: Penguin, 2000).

Hazlewood, P. *Marlborough School: Nurturing Independent Thinkers.* RSA Opening Minds Project (Stafford: Network Educational Press, 2005).

James, O. *Affluenza* (London: Random House, 2007).

Jensen, E. *The Learning Brain* (Del Mar, CA: Turning Point, 1995).

Lehrer, J. *The Decisive Moment: How the Brain Makes Up Its Mind* (Edinburgh: Canon Gate, 2009).

MacClean, P. *The Triune Brain in Evolution* (New York: Plenum, 1990).

Middlewood, D., Parker, R. and Beere, J. *Creating a Learning School* (London: Paul Chapman, 2005).

Prashnig, B. *Learning Styles in Action* (Stafford: Network Educational Press, 2006).

Robertson, I. *Mind Sculpture: Your Brain's Untapped Potential* (New York: Bantum Books, 1999).

Royal Society of Arts. *Opening Minds: Giving Young People a Better Chance* (London: RSA, 2005).

Ryan, W. *Leadership with a Moral Purpose* (Carmarthen: Crown House, 2009).

Seligman, M. E. P. *Authentic Happiness* (New York: Free Press, 2002).

Seligman, M. E. P., Reivich, K., Jaycox, L. and Gillham, J. *The Optimistic Child* (New York: Harper Perennial, 1995).

Wiliam, D. and Black, P. *Inside the Black Box* (London: NFER Nelson, 2006).

Useful websites

www.campaignforlearning.org

www.curriculumfoundation.org

www.curriculumqca.org.uk

www.dcsf.gov.ukprimarycurriculumreview

www.jackiebeere.com

www.openingminds.org.uk

www.qcda.org.uk

www.sage.pub.co.uk

www.theRSA.org

Index

The Independent Thinking Series brings together some of the most innovative practitioners working in education today under the guidance of Ian Gilbert, founder of Independent Thinking Ltd. www.independentthinking.co.uk

The Big Book of Independent Thinking: Do things no one does or do things everyone does in a way no one does — Edited by Ian Gilbert
ISBN 978-190442438-3

Little Owl's Book of Thinking: An Introduction to Thinking Skills — Ian Gilbert
ISBN 978-190442435-2

The Little Book of Thunks: 260 questions to make your brain go ouch! — Ian Gilbert
ISBN 978-184590062-5

The Buzz: A practical confidence builder for teenagers — David Hodgson
ISBN 978-190442481-9

Essential Motivation in the Classroom — Ian Gilbert
ISBN 978-041526619-2

Are You Dropping the Baton?: How schools can work together to get transition right
— Dave Harris Edited by Ian Gilbert
ISBN 978-184590081-6

Leadership with a Moral Purpose: Turning Your School Inside Out — Will Ryan Edited by Ian Gilbert
ISBN 978-184590084-7

The Little Book of Big Stuff about the Brain — Andrew Curran Edited by Ian Gilbert
ISBN 978-184590085-4

Rocket Up Your Class!: 101 high impact activities to start, end and break up lessons —
Dave Keeling Edited by Ian Gilbert
ISBN 978-184590134-9

The Lazy Teacher's Handbook: How Your Students Learn More When You Teach Less —
Jim Smith Edited by Ian Gilbert
ISBN 978-184590289-6

The Learner's Toolkit: Developing Emotional Intelligence, Instilling Values for Life, Creating Independent Learners and Supporting the SEAL Framework for Secondary Schools —
Jackie Beere Edited by Ian Gilbert
ISBN 978-184590070-0

The Little Book of Charisma: Applying the Art and Science — David Hodgson Edited by Ian Gilbert
ISBN 978-184590293-3

The Little Book of Inspirational Teaching Activities: Bringing NLP into the Classroom —
David Hodgson Edited by Ian Gilbert
ISBN 978-184590136-3

The Little Book of Music for the Classroom: Using Music to Improve Memory, Motivation, Learning and Creativity — Nina Jackson Edited by Ian Gilbert
ISBN 978-184590091-5

The Little Book of Values: Educating children to become thinking, responsible and caring citizens — Julie Duckworth Edited by Ian Gilbert
ISBN 978-184590135-6

The Primary Learner's Toolkit — Jackie Beere Edited by Ian Gilbert
ISBN 978-184590395-4

www.independentthinking.co.uk   www.crownhouse.co.uk

Jackie has written two books for secondary schools:

The Competency Curriculum Toolkit

Developing the PLTS Framework Through Themed Learning

Jackie Beere and Helen Boyle

ISBN 978-184590126-4

This book explores the concept of a competency-based curriculum for KS3 and provides a range of resources for implementing creative learning in schools. It is widely acknowledged that students will need to be flexible, self-motivated learners if they are to thrive in our rapidly changing global community.

- Do students need to nurture their resilience and commitment to learning?
- Are schools keen to develop the skills and competencies of learning how to learn, leadership and teamwork ready for their crucial choices in KS4?
- Can we help students become more resilient and self-reliant by teaching a project-based approach that delivers progress in key personal competencies?

Various models for delivery and assessment are considered and schemes of work for projects as well as sample lessons to use in the classroom are provided. In addition, the CD-ROM has a range of PowerPoint presentations for training staff and students. An essential toolkit for all those wishing to develop independent learners.

The Learner's Toolkit

Developing Emotional Intelligence, Instilling Values for Life, Creating Independent Learners and Supporting the SEAL Framework for Secondary Schools

Jackie Beere Edited by Ian Gilbert

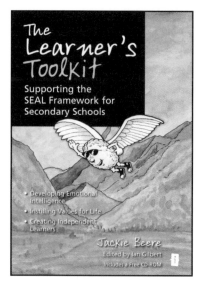

ISBN 978-184590070-0

The Learner's Toolkit an essential resource for supporting the SEAL framework in secondary schools and for all those teaching 11-16 year olds. It contains everything you need to create truly independent learners, confident and resilient in their ability to learn and learn well. The book contains 50 lessons to teach 50 competencies. Each has teacher's notes on leading the lesson and a CD-ROM in the back of the book has all the student forms and worksheets necessary for the lessons. Lessons include:

- getting to know yourself
- taking responsibility for your own life
- persistence and resilience
- setting goals for life
- controlling moods
- caring for your mind and body
- building brain power
- asking questions
- developing willpower
- pushing yourself out of your comfort zone
- prioritising and planning

Possessing these vital competencies will help students learn better and be able to contribute more effectively in school. It will also enable them to thrive in the increasingly fast-paced world of the 21st Century.

The Learner's Toolkit Student Workbook 1

The Habits of Emotional Intelligence

The Learner's Toolkit Student Workbook 2

Lessons in Learning to Learn: Values for Success in Life

Jackie Beere Edited by Ian Gilbert

ISBN 978-184590097-7

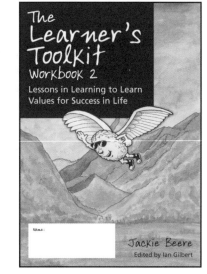

ISBN 978-184590103-5

To accompany *The Learner's Toolkit – Teacher's Resource*. These workbooks are designed for students to keep personal records of their work towards developing competencies in Learning, Emotional Intelligence and Values for Life. They are an outstanding resource for supporting the SEAL framework in secondary schools.

Workbook 1 includes lessons on:

- Getting to know yourself
- Taking responsibility for your own life
- Building confidence
- Persistence and resilience
- Setting goals for life
- Controlling moods
- Caring for mind and body
- Optimism
- Stress management
- Thinking skills
- Communication and cooperation

Workbook 2 Includes lessons on :

- How your brain works
- Multiple intelligences
- How to use your senses for learning
- Democracy and equality
- Attitude
- Love and understanding
- Social intelligence
- Forgiveness and fairness
- Empathy

Available as single copies or classroom packs – see www.crownhouse.co.uk for details